The Photoshop Elements 8 PocketGuide

Brie **Gyncild**

Ginormous knowledge, pocket-sized.

Peachpit Press

The Photoshop Elements 8 Pocket Guide
Brie Gyncild

Peachpit Press
1249 Eighth Street
Berkeley, CA 94710
510/524-2178
510/524-2221 (fax)

Find us on the Web at: www.peachpit.com
To report errors, please send a note to: errata@peachpit.com

Peachpit Press is a division of Pearson Education.

Editor: Rebecca Gulick
Copy Editor: Scout Festa
Production Coordinator: Myrna Vladic
Compositor: Jerry Ballew
Indexer: Valerie Haynes Perry
Technical Reviewer: Joe Kissell
Cover and Interior Design: Peachpit Press

ISBN 13: 978-0-321-66952-0
ISBN 10:   0-321-66952-5

9 8 7 6 5 4 3 2 1

Printed and bound in the United States of America

Dedication

For Sandy, the real photographer in the family

Acknowledgments

Even little books require many hands. Several people toiled behind the scenes to make this book happen. I'm particularly grateful that they performed their magic so quickly and (to me) invisibly. Scout Festa ably copy edited the book; Myrna Vladic coordinated the production; Jerry Ballew put it all together; Valerie Haynes Perry provided the index; and Joe Kissell caught all the little technical things that make the difference between a useful book and an irritating one. I love working with Rebecca Gulick, who issued the initial invitation, got me the resources I needed, and kept all of us on task to produce this book efficiently and without drama.

Thank you to the wonderful people in my life who graciously allowed me to use photos of them as examples: Sandy, Kathryn, Brooke, Andrew, and Colleen. The cats and garden never gave explicit permission, but I'm blessed by their presence in and out of photos, as well.

I put in long hours on several days, which wouldn't have been possible without the understanding and flexibility of my partner, Sandy, and her visiting parents, Doña and Verne.

Thanks, everybody! Let's do it again sometime.

About the Author

Brie Gyncild aims to make technical information accessible to those who need it. She's written books on many Adobe applications, including Adobe Photoshop, Adobe InDesign, and Adobe After Effects. Brie lives in Seattle with her partner, their cats, and an overgrown garden.

Contents

1

Meet Photoshop Elements

Adobe Photoshop Elements 8.0 marries sophisticated capabilities with a user-friendly interface. That's why it's a good choice for just about anyone who wants to enhance and improve their photos. The power of Adobe Photoshop CS4 lies beneath the surface, allowing you to correct lighting problems, remove ubiquitous red eye, and repair tears and stains in treasured heirloom photos.

A wide range of filters make it easy to give Aunt Sally a neon glow or turn an ocean snapshot into a captivating mosaic. And numerous features let you change your reality a little—or a lot. You can tweak group photos to capture everyone's best expressions, or move the whole set from a boring conference room to a sandy beach!

Differences in Windows and Mac OS versions

The editing functionality in Photoshop Elements is basically the same on Windows and on Mac OS. On both platforms, you can perform quick fixes, apply filters, or use advanced editing techniques. The only differences you're likely to encounter between the two are in keyboard shortcuts. (Where you press Command on the Mac, press Ctrl in Windows; for Option on the Mac, think Alt in Windows.)

Beyond editing functions, however, the programs differ quite a bit. Photoshop Elements for Windows includes a powerful image management tool called the Organizer. You can use the Organizer to tag, sort, search, and share images. You won't find the Organizer in Photoshop Elements for Mac. Most folks on the Mac are already using iPhoto or Aperture to manage their images, but if you haven't adopted one of those applications yet, you can use Adobe Bridge, which is installed with Photoshop Elements for Mac.

Some features, such as automatically sharing photos to Photoshop.com and purchasing prints online, are not available without the Organizer. However, you can upload files to Photoshop.com without using Photoshop Elements, so it's worth checking out if you're using Mac OS, too.

Because the Organizer is an integral part of Photoshop Elements for Windows, this book covers it in some detail in Chapter 2. If you're using Mac OS, Chapter 3 will get you up and running in Bridge, but it's not quite as comprehensive. If you're using iPhoto or Aperture, you've probably already got a system that works for you, so you can skip chapters 2 and 3.

The Welcome mat

When you first start the application, Photoshop Elements greets you with a Welcome screen. What you see depends on whether you're working in Mac OS or Windows—and in Windows, it depends on whether you've created a Photoshop.com account or not.

On the Mac, the Welcome screen contains buttons for importing an image or starting a new file from scratch. It'll open every time you start Photoshop Elements unless you tell it to do otherwise. If you want to skip this window when you start the application, deselect Show at Startup in the lower-right corner.

Figure 1.1
The Welcome screen in Mac OS offers buttons to get you started.

In Windows, the Welcome screen is quite different. Organize and Edit buttons are prominent, linking to the Organizer and Editor, of course. Additionally, you can create an Adobe ID if you don't already have one, and then log on to claim Photoshop.com membership.

Figure 1.2 *The Welcome screen in Windows invites you to create an Adobe ID if you don't have one.*

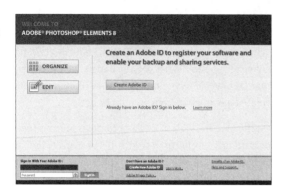

Once you have a Photoshop.com membership, the Welcome screen gives you information about your account. It also invites you to tour Photoshop Elements features, or to access tips and tricks in the Adobe Elements Inspiration Browser.

Figure 1.3
The Welcome screen changes after you have a Photoshop.com account.

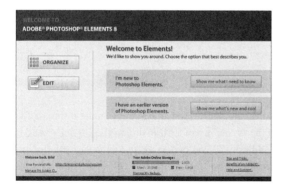

Photoshop.com membership

Photoshop.com is a file-sharing site, available for free to Photoshop Elements users in the United States. Free membership gives you 2 GB of free storage space for your photos, so you can share them with friends and family online. You can also download tutorials from the Inspiration Browser, and receive updated tips, templates, and art to use in Photoshop Elements.

Figure 1.4
Share your photos with family and friends on Photoshop.com

It's easiest to create a Photoshop.com membership through Photoshop Elements for Windows. In fact, the application practically begs you to do so. There's no such invitation in Mac OS, but you can create a Photoshop.com account on your own.

To create a Photoshop.com membership, you'll need an Adobe ID.

If you've ever purchased anything from the Adobe store online, used Acrobat.com, or posted to an Adobe user forum, you probably already have an Adobe ID. If you don't have one, it's easy and free to get one, and you can use it any time you access an Adobe service on the web.

In Windows, click the Create Adobe ID button in the Welcome screen, or log in at the bottom of the screen if you already have an Adobe ID. Then follow the onscreen instructions to create a Photoshop.com account.

In Mac OS, go to www.photoshop.com in a web browser. Click Join/Get Started, and follow the onscreen instructions to set up an account. Though you can't upload photos directly from Photoshop Elements on a Mac, you can upload them using Photoshop.com. You'll just need to know where to find them on your hard drive.

If 2 GB isn't enough space for your photos, you can purchase additional storage space. Or you can upgrade to a paid Premium membership. As you use Photoshop.com, you'll have plenty of opportunities to upgrade to Premium. You can choose to upgrade at any time, though, by clicking My Account and then Upgrade.

Changing Welcome screen settings (in Windows)

By default, each time you open Photoshop Elements in Windows, it displays the Welcome screen. You can then choose whether to open the Editor or the Organizer. But you can change those settings. You don't have a lot of options, but you can instruct the application to always open both the Welcome screen and the Organizer or the Welcome screen and the Editor. To make those changes, click the menu button in the upper-right corner of the Welcome screen ▤ . Then, make your choice and click OK.

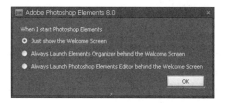

Figure 1.5 *You can automatically open the Editor or the Organizer along with the Welcome screen.*

There's no way to keep the Welcome screen from opening every time you start the application in Windows. Without it, Photoshop Elements has no way of knowing whether you want to open the Editor or the Organizer. If I had my druthers, there'd be some way to set a default so you could bypass the Welcome screen altogether. But there isn't. The good news is that the Welcome screen closes after you proceed to the Editor or the Organizer, so it's not taking up computer power. You can open it again from either workspace by clicking the Welcome Screen button 🏠 at the top of the window.

Importing photos

You need to get the photos into Photoshop Elements before you can perform any magic, or even any mundane tasks. How you import photos depends on whether you're using Mac OS or Windows, and where those photos are to begin with. You can import photos from cameras, card readers, CDs, DVDs, scanners, folders on your hard drive, and even mobile phone cameras.

Importing files in Windows

You can open photo files directly in the Editor. But it's better practice to import them into the Organizer first, where you can keep track of changes you make, group similar images, apply tags, search for specific photos, and otherwise keep your photo files in order. Chapter 2 goes into detail on working within the Organizer. But first you need to let the Organizer know your photos exist.

When you import photos into the Organizer, the actual photo files remain where they are on your computer hard drive. The Organizer catalog contains thumbnails, metadata (such as keywords you attach to the files), and references to the actual files.

From your hard drive

If your photos are already on your computer hard drive, it's a simple task to import them into the Organizer.

1. In the Organizer, choose File > Get Photos and Videos > From Files and Folders.

2. In the Get Photos and Videos from Files and Folders dialog box, navigate to the individual files or to the folder that contains the files you want to import.

3. Select one or more files, or one or more folders. (Ctrl-click to select multiple files or folders.) If you want to include all the files in all the folders within a selected folder, select Get Photos From Subfolders.

4. Click Get Media.

Figure 1.6

Select the files or folders you want to import, and click Get Media.

Photoshop Elements imports the files and displays them in the Photo Browser in the Organizer. In fact, the only files it shows are the ones you just imported. To see everything in your catalog, click Show All at the top of the Photo Browser.

From a camera or card reader

It's pretty easy to import photos from a camera or card reader. The Adobe Downloader is built in to Photoshop Elements to handle the task. When you download the images, they're copied to a folder on your hard drive and then imported into the Organizer.

1. Connect your camera or card reader to your computer. You'll probably need to either use a USB cable or remove a memory card and insert it into a card slot on your computer. If you're not sure how to connect your device to the computer, you'll need to check its documentation.

   Windows should display a dialog box asking you what you want to do with the files on the camera or card. You could just copy them to a folder or use another application to download them, but to have quick access to them in Photoshop Elements, you want to select the Organizer.

Figure 1.7 *When Windows asks you what to do, select Organize and Edit using Adobe Elements Organizer 8.0.*

2. Select Organize and Edit using Adobe Elements Organizer 8.0, and click OK.

tip If you always want to import photos directly into the Organizer, select "Always do the selected action" at the bottom of the Windows auto-play dialog box.

The Elements Organizer Photo Downloader dialog box appears. You can set up folders for the photos, rename them, and preview them using this dialog box.

Figure 1.8 *The Photo Downloader dialog box*

3. In the Photo Downloader dialog box, select a folder or subfolder for the photos, and a naming convention, if you want to.

> **tip** Many cameras name files with somewhat cryptic numbers. If you're downloading a set of photos from a birthday party, for example, you might want to rename the files with a base name of "J_birthday" and a starting number for the images. Then you'll get J_birthday1.jpg, J_birthday2.jpg, and so on, and you'll be able to identify the photos more easily.

4. Choose whether to delete the photos from your camera after they're downloaded, or to leave them on the camera or card. Any photos you choose not to download remain on the camera or card no matter which option you choose.

5. Click Advanced Dialog to see thumbnails of the photos and select which ones you want to download. You can also apply metadata such as keywords, and even automatically fix red eye.

Figure 1.9 *With the Advanced Dialog options, you can select which pictures to download.*

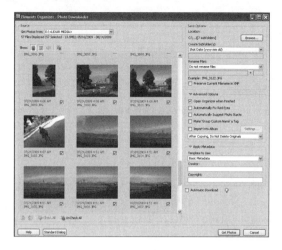

note In Windows Vista, if your camera is connected in PTP mode you may not be able to view camera raw or video files in the Photo Downloader. Try connecting your camera in USB Mass Storage mode or removing the card from the camera and using a card reader to connect it to your computer.

6. Select the photos you want to download, and any other options. Then, click Get Photos.

   The Photo Downloader copies the files to your hard drive, and deletes the selected photos from your camera or card reader if you selected that option.

7. Click Yes in the File Successfully Copied dialog box to see only the photos you just downloaded in Media Browser.

CAUTION: Remember that the photos themselves are stored in folders on your hard drive, and that the Organizer displays thumbnails that reference those original photos. If you delete the photos from your hard drive, the thumbnails in the Organizer lose their connection and contain very little data.

If you aren't having any luck, try plugging the camera into a different USB port, or use a card reader instead. Or, try copying the photos to your hard drive first and then importing them into Photoshop Elements.

tip **Don't want to go through all of this every time? If you select Automatic Download in the Photo Downloader dialog box, the Photo Downloader will download images any time a device is connected to your computer, using the settings in Preferences in the Organizer.**

From a scanner

Importing photos from a scanner is similar to importing files from a camera or card reader, but the scanner can scan in only one page at a time. You can put multiple images on a page and separate them later in Photoshop Elements.

1. Make sure your scanner is connected and installed for your computer. For help, you'll need to check your scanner documentation.

2. In the Organizer, choose File > Get Photos and Videos > From Scanner.

3. Select your scanner from the Scanner menu, and then select the folder for the resulting files on your hard drive. You can also set image quality, which will determine the file size. (Better quality = bigger file size.) And you can automatically fix red eye.

4. Click OK.

   What you see next depends on the type of driver your scanner uses. If it uses a TWAIN driver, Photoshop Elements launches the driver that came with your scanner. You may see the Windows XP scanning inter-face if you're using Windows XP with a WIA (Windows Imaging Architecture) scanner.

5. Select options in the scanner dialog box that appears, and follow any onscreen instructions. After the photo is scanned, a preview of the scan appears in the Getting Photos dialog box, and Photoshop Elements assigns the import date to the photos.

As with importing images from a card reader, Photoshop Elements places the images in files on your hard drive and then imports references into the Organizer.

From a mobile phone

Whether you can import photos from your phone depends on the file format your phone saves images in. To find out what format your phone uses, refer to the phone documentation.

Typically, you can transfer photos from a phone using either the Photo Downloader (as you would from a camera or card reader) or a cable or wireless transfer to your hard drive.

If your phone is compliant with NOKIA PC Suite 6.5 or higher, or if it stores photos on a removable flash or memory card, you can bring photos from your phone directly into Photoshop Elements using the Adobe Photo Downloader. Insert the card into your card reader, and then follow the instructions for downloading photos from a camera or card reader.

To use a cable or wireless transfer, you're going to have to look for instructions with your phone or from your phone manufacturer. Or just give it a try: for some phones, the Photo Downloader appears automatically when you connect via cable or wireless.

If you can transfer photos to your hard disk, import the photos into Organizer just as you would any other photos on your computer.

Mobile phone technology changes quickly. If you have an older phone, or a phone that uses a proprietary image format, you may not be able to import the photos at all. However, the latest phones make it easier to download photos for sharing on the Internet and elsewhere. If you're not sure how to get photos from your phone, your best bet is to contact your phone manufacturer or look for information on the Adobe website (www.adobe.com).

From a CD or DVD

Importing files from a CD or DVD isn't much different from importing files from your hard drive. The only difference is that Photoshop Elements will copy the files to your hard drive for you.

1. Pop the CD or DVD into your CD or DVD drive.

2. In the Organizer, choose File > Get Photos and Videos > From Files and Folders.

3. Navigate to the CD or DVD drive, and then select the photos you want to copy.

4. Select Copy Files on Import at the bottom of the dialog box to copy a full-resolution version of the image onto your hard disk.

note For some images, the Generate Previews option may also be available. That option makes a low-resolution copy of the file. Generally, that's a bad idea, because you want as much data as possible when you're editing images.

Figure 1.10 *New options appear at the bottom of the Import Files and Folders dialog box when you select photos from a CD or DVD.*

5. Type a volume name if you want to remember which CD or DVD you imported the file from.

6. Select any other options you want, such as fixing red eye, and then click Get Media.

From a video

You can capture individual frames from a digital video if it's saved in a format Photoshop Elements supports. When you capture a frame, the photo file has the name of the video file plus a number (for example, myvideo1, myvideo2, and so on). You can import entire videos into the Organizer, but to capture individual frames as photos you must use the Editor.

You won't find many references to video in this book, but once you've captured a frame as a photo, you can treat it like you would any other photo file.

tip To capture frames from a broader range of video formats, make sure you've got the latest versions of QuickTime, Windows Media Player, and other standard video software installed.

1. In the Editor, choose File > Import > Frame From Video.

2. In the Frame From Video dialog box, click Browse and then navigate to the video that contains the frame you want to use.

Figure 1.11 *Capture a frame from a video as a still photo in the Editor.*

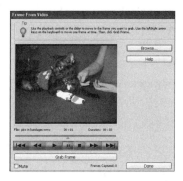

3. Click Open.

   The video you selected appears in the preview window.

4. Click the Play button to view the video. You can also move the slider to move to a particular point in the video.

5. When the frame you want to use appears, click Grab Frame or press the spacebar.

6. Grab any additional frames you want to use.

7. Click Done when you've grabbed all the frames you want to use. The frames you've selected are in separate windows in the Editor.

8. Choose File > Save to save each of the still images to a folder on your computer.

Importing photos in Mac OS

To edit images in Photoshop Elements in Mac OS, they must first be on your hard drive or on a CD or DVD. You can use the Photo Downloader to pull images from a camera, a card reader, or other locations into Adobe Bridge. The Adobe Photo Downloader is similar across Mac OS and Windows. Once you've imported the photos, you can open and edit them in Photoshop Elements. You can also scan directly into Photoshop Elements if your scanner uses a supported plug-in module.

From your hard drive

If your photos are already on your hard drive, you can open them directly in Photoshop Elements.

1. In Photoshop Elements, choose File > Open.

2. Select the photo or photos you want to work with, and click Open.

If you want to browse your photos before opening them, choose File > Browse With Bridge instead of File > Open.

You don't need to import files into Bridge from your hard drive. Bridge displays photos in their original folders.

From a camera or card reader

To import photos from a camera or card reader, first download them onto your hard drive into Adobe Bridge.

1. In Photoshop Elements, choose File > Adobe Photo Downloader.

 You can set Adobe Photo Downloader to launch automatically when you connect a camera or card reader to your computer. It will prompt you to do so when it opens.

2. Connect your camera or card reader to your computer. Most connect with a USB cord. Check the documentation that came with your camera or card reader for instructions if it isn't obvious.

3. In the Photo Downloader dialog box, choose your device from the Get Photos From menu if it isn't already listed.

Figure 1.12 *Use the Photo Downloader to import photos from a camera or card reader.*

4. Choose a folder for the photos. By default, Photo Downloader creates subfolders for the dates the photos were taken. You can change the subfolder configuration, though.

5. If you want to rename the individual photos, select a formula (such as shot date plus a custom name) and enter a custom name if appropriate.

6. Click Advanced Dialog to preview the photos and select which ones to download. You can also apply metadata, including copyright information.

Figure 1.13 *Preview and select specific images to download in the Advanced Dialog box.*

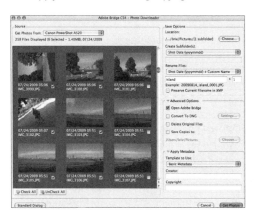

7. Click Get Photos.

Photo Downloader imports the photos you selected. To display the images in Adobe Bridge, select Open Adobe Bridge in the Photo Downloader dialog box before you click Get Photos.

From a mobile phone

How you import photos from a mobile phone depends on the phone. You'll need to look at the documentation for your phone to determine the best method. Typically, you'll use either a USB cord or Bluetooth to transfer data from the phone to your computer.

You may be able to use the Adobe Photo Downloader to download photos, or you may need to use an application that came with your phone.

From a scanner

If your scanner includes a plug-in module that is compatible with Photoshop Elements, scanning directly into the application is pretty straightforward.

1. Connect your scanner to your computer, if it isn't already connected, and install any software that comes with the scanner.

2. In Photoshop Elements, choose File > Import > [scanner name]. If your scanner doesn't have its own plug-in module but supports TWAIN, you may see a TWAIN option; you can select that.

3. Select a location for the scanned images and follow any onscreen instructions to set scanner settings. The options you see depend on whether you're using a scanner plug-in module or a TWAIN interface.

tip If Photoshop Elements doesn't recognize your scanner, use the software that came with your scanner to scan your images. For the best results, save your images as TIFF or JPEG files.

From a CD or DVD

Opening a file from a CD or a DVD is just like opening an image from your hard drive. The only trick is to make sure you save a copy to your hard drive.

1. Insert the CD or DVD into your drive.

2. In Photoshop Elements, choose File > Open.

3. Navigate to the photos or photos you want to work with.

4. Select the images and click Open.

5. Select each image and choose File > Save As. Navigate to the folder where you want to save the image. You can rename the image if you like. Then, click Save.

From a video

As in Windows, you can capture individual frames from a digital video if it's saved in a format Photoshop Elements supports. When you capture a frame, the photo file has the name of the video file plus a number (for example, myvideo1, myvideo2, and so on).

You won't find many references to video in this book, but once you've captured a frame as a photo, you can treat it like you would any other photo file.

1. In Photoshop Elements, choose File > Import > Frame From Video.

2. In the Frame From Video dialog box, click Browse and then navigate to the video that contains the frame you want to use.

3. Click Open.

   The video you selected appears in the preview window.

4. Click the Play button to view the video. You can also move the slider to move to a particular point in the video.

5. When the frame you want to use appears, click Grab Frame or press the spacebar.

6. Grab any additional frames you want to use.

7. Click Done when you've grabbed all the frames you want to use. The frames you've selected are in separate windows in Photoshop Elements.

8. Choose File > Save to save each of the still images to a folder on your computer.

2

Managing Images in Organizer

Got photos? Of course you do. Probably thousands of them, given how easy and inexpensive it is to snap an image using a digital camera or cell phone. The digital revolution has created a chaos of abundance. And that's not even counting all the older photos neatly arrayed in albums or, for most of us, stacked in shoeboxes in the closet.

If you're using Photoshop Elements for Windows, the Organizer makes your collection manageable. You can add keywords and captions, search for images that look similar, view images in a slide show, and perform other tasks that make it easier for you to find specific photos and share them with others.

note If you're using Photoshop Elements for Mac, you can accomplish many of the same organizational tasks in Adobe Bridge. See Chapter 3 to learn how.

When you first import images into the Organizer, only the images you just imported show up in the Media Browser. To view all the images in your catalog, click Show All at the top of the Media Browser. The catalog contains all the images you've imported into the Organizer. You can create multiple catalogs, but most people leave their files in one and then use albums, tags, and other methods to organize images.

The catalog contains information about your files, including their file names, any metadata attached to them, and their location on your disk. However, the actual files themselves never come into the Organizer; they stay wherever they are on your system. The Organizer displays only a thumbnail of each image in the Media Browser.

 tip To see the path to a file, right-click its thumbnail and choose Show Properties.

Viewing images

By default, the Organizer displays images in thumbnail view. To change the size of the thumbnails—and thus, the number of images you can view at a time—move the slider at the top of the window. When the slider is all the way to the right, you view just one image at a time.

In thumbnail view, images are displayed in order of date, either newest first or oldest first. You can change the order using the menu next to the thumbnail slider.

To view the file name and date, select Details.

Figure 2.1 *By default, the Organizer displays images in thumbnail view.*

Figure 2.2 *Move the slider to change the size of the thumbnails.*

Separating by import batch or folder

If you have a large number of photos, viewing them all by date may not be the most efficient way to browse. You can have the Organizer arrange them by the date and time you imported them. Of course, if you imported your entire collection at once, that won't help much.

To view photos according to when you imported them, select Import Batch from the Display menu at the top-right of the Organizer window.

Figures 2.3-2.4
You can separate imported batches of photos.

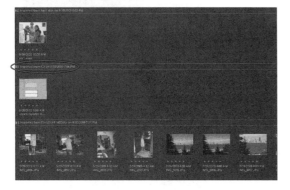

If you've organized your photos by folder on your hard drive, you might like to view them that way in the Organizer as well. To view photos by folder, choose Folder Location from the Display menu.

Photoshop Elements creates a folder tree on the left side, and then separates the folders in the Media Browser with horizontal dividers. When you select a folder on the left, the Media Browser jumps to those images. You can scroll up or down to see photos in other folders. It's not the most intuitive way to browse images, but once you understand the way it's set up, you can use it to quickly locate files when you know what folder you stashed them in.

Figures 2.5-2.6
*Scroll through
folders to find
the images you
want to work
with.*

Placing images in time

You can also view your images on a calendar, with photos on the dates
they were taken. For those who are both visual and gifted with a memory
for dates, Date View can be a great way to find images quickly. For others,
it's a good way to visualize a sequence of events.

- To view images in Date View, choose Date View from the Display menu.
  You can view by day, month, or year.

- Click Year, Month, or Day at the bottom of the window to change
  the display.

- To move forward through time, click the right arrow next to the month
  or year; to move backward, click the left arrow.

- To view all the images for the day, click Day and then use your right and left arrow keys to scroll through the images.

- To return to the original view, choose Media Browser from the Display menu.

Figure 2.7
See images in the context of time using Date View.

Mapping photos

To see photos in geographical context, you can also place them on a map using Yahoo Maps. Photoshop Elements places a red pin everywhere you attach photos; you can scroll around the state, country, or world, viewing images as you go.

To place photos on a map:

1. In the Organizer, select an image or group of images.

2. Choose Edit > Place on Map.

3. Enter the location—as precise as a street address or as vague as a country—and click Find.

4. Select your location, and then click OK in the Look Up Address dialog box.

To view images on the map, use the Hand tool to select a pin and see the photos beneath it.

Figure 2.8 *Put your photos on the map!*

To hide the map, choose Window > Show Map or just click the X in the upper-right corner. Choose Window > Show Map to see it again.

note You need to have Internet access to see the map. If you are not currently connected to the Internet, Photoshop Elements won't be able to find Yahoo Maps.

Filling the screen with each image

To focus on each individual image, view them in full-screen mode. As the image fills the screen, you can rotate it, apply several quick fixes (such as removing red eye), mark it for printing later, apply keywords, or delete it. Full-screen mode can be useful for reviewing images just after you've taken them.

The image fills the screen unless you display a filmstrip of the selected images, the Quick Organize panel, or the Quick Edit panel. A toolbar appears on the bottom of the screen when you move your mouse over it.

Quick Edits panel

filmstrip

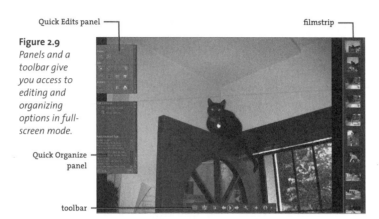

Figure 2.9
Panels and a toolbar give you access to editing and organizing options in full-screen mode.

Quick Organize panel

toolbar

- To enter full-screen mode, click the Full-Screen button at the top of the window.

- To view the next image in full-screen mode, press the right arrow key on your keyboard or click the right arrow in the toolbar.

- To leave full-screen mode, press Esc or click the X in the toolbar.

- Click the appropriate icon in the toolbar to show or hide the filmstrip, Quick Organize panel, or Quick Edit panel.

- To apply a keyword to the current image, select the keyword in the Quick Organize panel on the left side of the window. Applied keywords appear in white; all keywords are listed alphabetically.

- To perform edits or mark an image for printing, use the icons in the Quick Edit panel on the left side of the window.

Viewing a slide show

In full-screen mode, you can view the selected images in an instant slide show.

1. Click the Full-Screen button at the top of the Organizer window.

2. Click the Open Settings Dialog icon in the toolbar (it looks like a wrench).

3. Select the length of time each image stays on the screen, the background music, and other options. Click OK.

4. To set a transition, click the Transitions icon in the toolbar (it looks like an arrow in motion) and then select a transition style. (I'm fond of Pan and Zoom myself.) Click OK.

5. Press the Play icon in the toolbar to start the slide show. Press Esc when you want to stop the slide show.

Tagging photos

You can attach information to photos to make it easier for you to find them later. Rate images, apply keywords, or add captions to help you sort, search, and share images later.

Rating images

Some images are just better quality than others. And some images are favorites because they feature a favorite person or bring up memories of a special time. Photoshop Elements gives you the ability to rate images with one to five stars, but it's up to you what those stars mean—or whether you use them at all. Because you can search for images based on their star rating, that rating can be one way to sift through hundreds or thousands of images more quickly.

To rate an image, click the appropriate star beneath it. For example, to give an image a five-star rating, click the fifth star, and all five will become yellow. To give it three stars, click the middle star, and the first three stars are yellow. If you've selected multiple images, rating one applies the same rating to all of them.

Figure 2.10 *Rate an image with one to five stars.*

 You can also select an image and choose Edit > Ratings > [number of stars].

Using keywords

The most efficient way to organize your images in Photoshop Elements is to attach meaningful keywords to them. You can attach as many keywords to each image as you like. For example, you might include the names of the people in the photo, the location, and the event.

You can also categorize keywords to make them easier to sort. For example, I use a "cats" category for all the keywords that have to do with the felines in my life and in my photos. Within that category are keywords for each of their names, as well as keywords for kittens and other kinds of photos I might want to find. You can create any categories that are meaningful to you. Categories are handy because when you search for an entire category, you can find any image with any of that category's keywords attached.

Before you begin creating and applying keywords and categories, spend a few minutes thinking about your photo collection and how you like to use it. You may want to have categories for events, vacations, birthdays, places you've lived, or activities such as fishing. Additionally, all keywords and categories you create should be personally meaningful to you.

Developing a rough plan will help you create keywords and categories that you'll use more consistently, and that will save you frustration later.

Keywords are displayed in the Keyword Tags panel. By default, they're displayed hierarchically, in categories. To view all tags in alphabetical order, click the View Keyword Tag Cloud button at the top of the Keyword Tags panel.

Figure 2.11 *By default, keywords are displayed in categories.*

Figure 2.12 *You can also view them in a keyword tag cloud.*

Adding categories and keywords

To add a category, click the Plus sign in the Keyword Tags panel and choose New Category. Then, name the category and select a color for its tag. Click OK to create it.

Figure 2.13 *Add categories that work for you.*

To add a keyword, click the New button in the Keyword Tags panel and choose New Keyword Tag. Then, choose a category or subcategory for the keyword and name the keyword. Click OK.

When the keyword is first created, its icon is a generic question mark. The first time you attach a keyword to a photo, Photoshop Elements uses that photo for the keyword icon.

Figure 2.14 *At first, a keyword's icon is a question mark.*

Figure 2.15 *The first photo you apply the keyword to becomes the icon.*

Applying keywords

There are several ways to tag a photo with a keyword.

- Drag one or more photos from the Media Browser onto the keyword tag in the Keyword Tags panel.

- Drag the keyword tag onto a photo thumbnail or a selection of photos.

- Select one or more photos, and then choose a keyword from the Tag Selected Media menu in the Keyword Tags panel and click Apply.

- Select keywords to apply to photos as you view them in full-screen mode.

Finding faces

You can let Photoshop Elements find faces in your photos for you to tag.

1. Select the images you want to tag.

2. Choose Find > Find People For Tagging. (Or click the Start People Recognition button in the Keyword Tags panel.)

   Photoshop Elements displays each of your images with the faces bracketed.

3. Identify the face:

   If you see "Who is this?" try clicking the text: frequent keywords are listed there, and you may be able to just click the right one. Otherwise, type in the name.

   If Photoshop Elements recognizes the face, it will ask "Is this Brie?" for example. Click the green Commit button if it's correct, and the red X if it's not.

4. Click Done when you've finished, or click the arrow to go to the next face.

Figure 2.16 *Let Photoshop Elements find the faces for you to identify.*

Sometimes Photoshop Elements can misidentify faces. I've been asked to name kneecaps, doorframes, and other random objects. But you can easily tell Photoshop Elements that it isn't actually a face; just click the X in the upper-left corner of the box.

tip If you select Recognize People Automatically in the Auto-Analyzer Options panel of the Preferences dialog box, Photoshop Elements will present you with the question "Who is this?" whenever it finds a photo that hasn't been tagged with someone's name. To disable this feature, choose Edit > Preferences > Auto-Analyzer Options, and deselect Recognize People Automatically.

Attaching folder keywords instantly

You can automatically attach keyword tags to images based on the folders they're in.

1. Choose Folder Location from the Display menu.

2. Select the folder containing the photos you want to tag from the folder tree on the left side of the screen.

3. Click the Instant Keyword Tag button on the right side of the separator bar in the Media Browser—that's the bar that names the folder.

Figure 2.17 *Click the Instant Keyword Tag button to apply a keyword to all photos in a folder.*

All items in that folder are selected and the Create And Apply New Keyword Tag dialog box opens.

4. Choose a category or subcategory from the Category menu. You can also rename the keyword if the folder name wasn't as useful as it might have been.

5. Click OK. All the photos in that folder now have the keyword applied to them.

Auto-analyzing images

The Organizer includes a feature called the Auto-Analyzer, which analyzes images to identify photo quality, focus, faces, and other attributes. When you run the Auto-Analyzer, it attaches Smart Tags to your images to identify those qualities. By default, Auto-Analyzer is off. To run it, select the images you want to analyze and choose Edit > Run Auto-Analyzer. (To have it run automatically, change the setting in the Preferences dialog box.)

The idea is great. It can be very handy to see right away which are low-quality photos and which are high-quality, to identify blurred images and what kind of blur they have, or to see which images are too light or too dark. But I find the analysis suspect. This feature was really designed for Premiere Elements, and I'm betting it works better with video. You can run it to see if it gives you useful information, but I think most of us are better off making our own judgments about our images—and creating our own tags if we need to be able to search for low-quality or blurred images.

Adding captions

Captions can give context for a photo, but they're also useful for searching for images. You can display captions when you view the images in full-screen mode as part of a slide show; include them when you print images; and add them to projects such as online albums and photo books. Captions can be up to 2000 characters long, much longer than the 140 characters you can use in Twitter!

You can add a caption in several different ways:

■ Double-click a photo to display it in single-photo view, select Details, and then click the current caption or the text "Click here to add caption." Enter your caption. Click outside the textbox to accept the change.

Figure 2.18 *In single-photo view, click the caption field at the bottom of the window and then type a caption.*

■ Select a photo, and choose Edit > Add Caption. Then, type a caption and click OK.

■ Choose Window > Properties, and click the General button. Now, select an image and type a caption for it in the Caption textbox.

■ Select multiple files, and choose Edit > Add Caption To Selected Items. Then, type your caption and click OK. The same caption is applied to all the selected photos.

tip To add individual captions to several photos in a row, it's easiest to view the photos in single-photo view. Enter the caption on one, press Enter, and then press the arrow key to continue to the next image.

Searching for images

The purpose of organizing photos is to make it easy to find the one you're looking for. If you've applied keywords, added captions, and included other metadata, you'll have what you need to locate photos when you need them. You can also find photos if you know when they were taken, or if you gave them a star rating.

Finding photos using keywords

Tagging all your photos with keywords can be tedious, but this is where it pays off. Displaying photos with only the selected keywords is a very quick way to narrow down the number of photos you need to sift through to find the one you're looking for. Of course, this method is most effective if you've been savvy about assigning keywords.

- To show only those photos with a particular keyword, click the box next to the tag.

Figure 2.19 *Select a keyword to quickly narrow down your search.*

- To see photos with more than one keyword (for example, all the photos that have both "Allison" and "camping" applied), select the boxes next to each of the keywords.

 If you select a keyword category, all the photos with any of the keywords included in the category are shown.

- To see only photos that have a particular keyword, you can also type the keyword in the Search textbox at the top of the Organizer window.

Seeing stars

If you've rated your photos, you can search by star ratings. To view rated images, click a star rating at the top of the Organizer window. For example, if you want to view only images you rated four stars or higher, click the fourth star at the top of the window.

Figure 2.20
See only the images you've given specific star ratings.

You can combine a star-rating search with a keyword search. Select the keywords you require in the Keyword Tags panel, and then select a star rating at the top of the Organizer window. If you've selected "Allison" and "camping," and then select a star rating of four stars or more, only those photos with both keywords and a star rating of four or five will appear.

You can also choose to view only those photos with a specific star rating: choose Only from the menu after the stars. Or, you can look for photos with a star rating equal to or less than the one you specify: choose and lower from the menu to the right of the stars.

Homing in with metadata

You can locate photos using their captions, file names, edit or import dates, or other metadata. Just about any information attached to the photo is fair game for the Find command.

Choose Find, and then choose an option such as By Caption Or Note or By Details (Metadata). Enter the data you're looking for, and click OK or Search.

To search by the date the photo was imported, emailed, printed, or exported, choose Find > By History > [date type]. This is particularly handy if you're looking for the set of photos you printed last week!

Figure 2.21
Quickly find photos you printed on a specific date.

Viewing images on the timeline

If you know when a photo was taken, you can jump to it quickly using the timeline. (If the date the photo was taken isn't available to Photoshop Elements, it displays the photo at the point it was last edited.)

Choose Window > Timeline. A timeline appears across the top of the window, with images clumped in it.

Then, move the finder across the timeline to scroll quickly through images in the Media Browser to the date you're looking for. Or, click a point in the timeline to jump there in the Media Browser.

Figure 2.22 *Jump right to a moment in time to find your photos.*

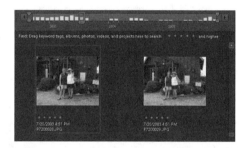

Using the Search textbox

The Search textbox at the top of the Organizer window is there for just about any kind of search you want to do. Enter a keyword, a word from a caption, a date, or any other information about the file, or any other information about the file..

Figure 2.23 *Enter a keyword, caption, date, or any other information about the file in the Search textbox.*

Finding similar photos

Photoshop Elements can attempt to locate photos that are similar to
the one you select. This can be an interesting place to start, especially if
you're looking for images of the same place that were taken at different
times. However, this isn't the fastest or most reliable way to find most
images. I'm not sure what criteria Photoshop Elements uses to determine
similarities, but I'm often entertained by the results. Photos taken of the
same subject in the same setting just 40 seconds apart can come up as
less similar than completely different subjects in different settings.

To have Photoshop Elements identify the photos it considers similar,
select an image and then choose Find > By Visual Similarity With Selected
Photos and Videos. The Organizer displays images its analysis found to be
similar to the one you selected, and it displays the percentage of similarity at the top of the image.

Figure 2.24 *Finding
similar photos can
yield interesting
results.*

Keeping things tidy

Most of us have too many photos. I know I certainly do. And I'm not
about to part with any of them. You can find individual pictures when
you're looking for them, but how can you rein in the chaos the rest of
the time? Photoshop Elements offers three features that can keep things
a little tidier: albums, version sets, and stacks.

Creating albums

In the old days (you know, a decade ago), we used to put our photos in things called photo albums. These were books that had a few photos on each page, sometimes with handwritten or typed pieces of paper stuck in with them to explain what was going on. In most houses, these albums were lined up on bookshelves or stacked in precarious piles on coffee table shelves, and when someone got to reminiscing, they'd come out for a nice trip down memory lane.

You can create similar albums in the digital world, with captions and everything. You never have to dust them, and you can share them with friends, relatives, or new acquaintances who are far from your living room.

In many cases, the easiest way to organize photo albums is by event. You might create one for the pictures from an office party, a vacation, or the birth of a grandchild. You could also create separate albums for different people in your life, or to show off how your garden has progressed over the years. Really, you can create an album arranged around any theme that makes sense to you. And a single photo can be included in several different albums. Photoshop Elements adds a green square tag to the thumbnails of images included in albums.

One of the benefits of albums is that Photoshop Elements can automatically back them up to Photoshop.com for you. It can't back up photos that aren't in albums.

Albums can be grouped into categories. You can wait and create categories after you have several albums, so that you can see what patterns make sense. Or if you already know what kind of albums you want to create, you can set up categories ahead of time. For example, you might set up categories for family gatherings, vacations, home, or friends.

- To create a category, click the New button at the top of the Albums panel and then choose New Album Category. Name the category, and if it's a subcategory, select a parent category. (If it's not a subcategory, choose None (Top Level) for the parent category.) Then, click OK.

Figure 2.25
Categories keep albums organized.

- To create a new album, click the New button at the top of the Albums panel and then choose New Album. Name the album, select a category, and start dragging photos into the album. If you want to automatically back up your album on Photoshop.com, select Backup/Synchronize. Click Done when you've finished.

Figure 2.26
Albums let you easily group photos by theme.

tip If you want to share your albums on Photoshop.com, you can use an online photo album template that gives it more of the feel of a coffee table book. To do that, click the Share tab and select Online Album. (Skip ahead to Chapter 9 for more information about it.)

- To view an album, click its name in the Albums panel.

Figure 2.27 *To see the photos in an album, select it in the Albums panel.*

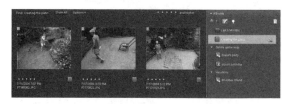

- To create an album from images you've found in a search, click the New button in the Albums panel and choose New Album. All visible photos are automatically added to the album.

- To automatically add photos you're downloading to a new album, click Advanced Dialog in the Photo Downloader. Then, select Import Into Album. Click Settings and then Create New Album. Name the album, and click OK to download the photos directly into their own album.

note When Photoshop Elements creates albums, it doesn't actually move any files around on your hard drive. It just adds another reference to them.

Stacking images

Just as you might stack related photos in the real world, you can group similar photos in stacks in the Organizer. Stacking photos takes up less space and removes visual clutter in the Media Browser. I find stacks especially useful if I've taken multiple shots of the same thing, hoping to get just the right facial expressions or lighting.

- To create a stack, select the images you want to stack and then choose Edit > Stack > Stack Selected Photos. Only one of the photos appears in the Media Browser, but the icon in the right corner tells you it's a stack.

- To see all the images in a stack, right-click the stack and choose Stack > Expand Photos In Stack. Photos in a stack share a continuous gray background.

- To stack images again, right-click and choose Stack > Collapse Photos In Stack.

Figure 2.28 *Six photos have been stacked so that only one is displayed.*

Figure 2.29 *When the stack is expanded, the six images share a common background.*

Saving version sets

A version set is a specific kind of stack. It contains an original photo along with edited iterations of the photo. Saving edited versions in a version set makes it easier to see how the image has changed, and to return to an earlier draft.

Edits you make using Quick Fixes are automatically added to version sets. To include other edited versions in a version set, choose File > Save As in the Editor. Then, in the Save As dialog box, select Save In Version Set With Original.

3

Managing Images in Bridge (Mac OS)

You don't have to organize your photos in order to edit them in Photoshop Elements. But if you don't organize your photos somewhere, you can easily spend hours at a time trying to track down the image you're looking for—and that takes away from the fun of editing.

Adobe Bridge CS4 is a file organization tool that is included with most Adobe applications. Using Bridge, you can add metadata, including keywords and ratings, to images. That metadata makes it easier to search for particular photos later. You can also keep Bridge tidier by stacking similar files, so that only one of the thumbnails is displayed.

Figure 3.1
Adobe Bridge helps you manage your images.

You can use any application you like to organize your images. If you're happy with iPhoto, Aperture, or another application, there's no reason to change. But if you aren't using another application, Bridge can help you corral your photos before they get out of control. And when it's easier to find your images, you can spend more of your time making them great.

Viewing images in Bridge

By default, Bridge opens in the Essentials workspace, which includes panels for navigating folders, filtering files, and viewing and applying metadata and keywords. It also includes the Content panel in the middle of the screen—that's where it displays thumbnails of your images. The Preview panel in the upper-right corner displays the preview of the image or images you've selected in the Content panel.

To change the size of the thumbnails in the Content panel, drag the thumbnail slider at the bottom of the window. You can also change the sizes of any of the panels by dragging the dividers between them.

You can select a different workspace, if you like, or customize the workspace to suit your needs. Workspaces are designed to arrange panels appropriately for various tasks, such as working with metadata or keywords, printing or creating web galleries (use the Output workspace for those tasks), and so on. To change the workspace, choose Window > Workspace > [workspace].

 When I give instructions for Bridge, I assume you're using the Essentials workspace unless otherwise noted.

Navigating folders

In some ways, Bridge is similar to the Finder. You can copy, move, or even delete the actual files and folders on your system in Bridge. You'll be prompted to confirm deletion, but it's still a good idea to be careful. If you delete something from Bridge, you're deleting it from your computer.

- To navigate to a particular folder or file, select a folder in the Folders panel or the Favorites panel.

- Click the Go Back and Go Forward buttons in the path bar to move up or down a level.

- Double-click a folder in the Content panel to open it and see its contents.

 If you want to see all the contents of a folder, including the subfolders, choose View > Show Items From Subfolders.

Sorting images

By default, files are shown in the Content pane in alphabetical order by file name. But you can sort them using other criteria, including creation date, rating, dimensions, or even resolution. You can even sort them manually if you have a hankering to drag images into a different order.

To change the sorting order, choose View > Sort > [sort option].

Figure 3.2 *You can change the sorting order in Bridge.*

If you opt to sort files manually, drag a file where you want it. When you see a bar between files, drop the file in place.

 You can drag files into a different order even if you haven't chosen Manually from the menu!

Viewing a slide show

You can view a set of images as a full-screen slide show almost instantly in Bridge.

1. Select the images you want to show. If no images are selected, Bridge will use all the files in the folder (including non-image files or folders) in the slide show.

2. Choose View > Slideshow Options.

3. In the Slideshow Options dialog box, set options for slide duration, captions, and transitions. Then click Play.

Captions in the slide show include the file name or page numbers. You cannot add separate captions to your images in Bridge.

Figure 13.3 *Bridge uses the options you set for any slide show you play until you change them.*

 Once you've selected the options you want to use, you don't need to set them every time. Just select the images for the slide show, and then choose View > Slideshow.

Tagging photos

Attaching ratings, labels, or keywords to images makes it easier to find them later.

Rating and labeling images

In Bridge, you can assign star ratings to images, or label them with colors.

How you use the star ratings is up to you. You might use them to identify the quality of the photography. Or they could indicate how much you like a particular photo, or even how useful a photo might be in a particular project you're working on.

In addition to colors, you can add text to labels to make their meaning clearer for you. You could use labels to distinguish between photos you want to keep digitally, images you want to print, those you want to delete, and others that you want to share with friends or family. It's up to you how you use labels; they're there to make your life easier.

To assign ratings, select one or more images and choose Label > [rating], or select an image and click the appropriate dot beneath it.

To apply a label, select one or more images and choose Label > [label].

Figures 3.04-3.05
You can apply a rating, a label, or both to an image.

 You can label and rate folders, too!

To change the name of a label, choose Adobe Bridge CS4 > Preferences and then select Labels from the list on the left. Type a name for each of the labels.

 When you change the name of a label, files with the original label appear with white labels in the Content panel.

Adding keywords

Keywords are another great tool for sifting through thousands of photos quickly. You can create keywords to identify individual people, events, places, photo qualities, or anything else that is meaningful to you. In Bridge, keywords appear in the Keywords panel. You can also create categories for keywords, which then appear in a hierarchy.

- To create a new keyword, select a keyword on the same level as thone you want to add. Then, click the New Keyword button in the Keywords panel, name the keyword, and press Return.

 If you want to create a category that can't itself be applied to files, put its name in brackets, like this: [Category name].

- To apply a keyword to a file, select the file and then click the check box next to the keyword in the Keywords panel. Bridge displays a check mark next to keywords that are applied to the selected file.

Figure 3.6 *Apply keywords to an image to make it easier to find later.*

Searching for images

Here's where the work you put into rating images, labeling them, and adding keywords pays off. If you use keywords, ratings, and labels that are personally meaningful to you, you should be able to narrow down your images to find the one you're looking for quickly.

Weeding out the riffraff with ratings and labels

You can see only the files with a particular number of stars in their ratings, or a combination of files with, say, three stars and four stars. You can view only the files with a particular label, or select a few label colors to display. And you can mix and match. Perhaps you want to show only the images that have a blue label and four stars, for example. The Filters panel makes it all possible.

- To view only the images with a particular rating, select that rating in the Filters panel. A check mark next to a rating indicates that it's used in the filtering criteria.

- To view only the images with a particular label, select that label in the Filters panel. Again, a check mark means the label is being used to filter the images.

Figure 3.7 *Use the Filters panel to limit images to those with a particular rating or label.*

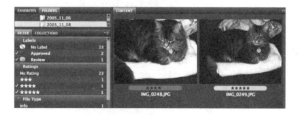

- To see all the images in a folder, but sort them according to their labels or ratings, choose View > Sort > By Label or View > Sort > By Rating.

Finding keywords and other metadata

The Filters panel can also show or hide images based on their keywords or other metadata. Selecting multiple keywords displays files that contain any of the selected keywords. The same is true in any other category, such as labels or ratings or file types. However, if you select criteria in different categories, only files that meet the criteria in all categories are displayed.

You can also find files that include specific keywords or other metadata using the Find command. Choose Edit > Find. In the Find dialog box, enter your search criteria. You can find files based on any metadata, including keywords.

Using the Search textbox

Don't overlook the Search textbox in the upper-right corner of the Bridge window. You can cut right to the chase and enter your search criteria there, press Return, and Bridge will search the selected folder and its subfolders for files that have your criteria in any of their metadata.

Grouping images

Sometimes you want to browse through images of a theme, whether they are from a particular event or chart a child's growth over the years. You can create collections in Bridge to pull together images that aren't all in a single folder. You can also stack similar images, so that they don't clutter up the Content panel as you're viewing your images.

Creating collections

Collections can contain images from several different folders, grouped together for easy viewing. You can create collections manually, adding the images you want to include. You can also create collections automatically, including all the images you found when you performed a search. The Collections panel is the place to create and open collections.

- To create a collection, click the New Collection button at the bottom of the Collections panel. Then, name it, and start dragging photos onto it.

tip The only indication Bridge offers that you've added the photo to the collection is that the collection name has a colored border when you drop the photo onto it. To reassure yourself of the collection's contents, double-click it to open it.

- To create a collection from selected images, select them in the Content panel and then click the New Collection button in the Collections panel. Click Yes when Bridge asks whether you want to include the selected files in the new collection.

- To view a collection, click its name in the Collections panel.

Figure 3.8
Collections can include photos from many different folders.

- To add files to an existing collection, drag them onto the collection name in the Collections panel. You can drag them from the Content panel or the Finder.

- To remove a file from a collection, open the collection and select the file in the Content panel. Click Remove From Collection in the Content panel.

- To create a smart collection, click the New Smart Collection button at the bottom of the Collections panel. Then, in the Smart Collection dialog box, enter the search criteria for the images you want to include in the collection.

Stacking images

Stacking photos takes up less space and removes visual clutter in the Content panel. I find stacks especially useful if I've taken multiple shots of the same thing, hoping to get just the right facial expressions or lighting. You can also use stacks to organize image sequences.

Anything you could do to a single file, you can also do to a stack. For example, you can apply a rating to a stack. If the stack is expanded, the same rating applies to all files in the stack. If the stack is collapsed, the rating typically applies to only the top file in the stack. However, if you click the stack border, it applies to all files in the stack.

- To stack images, select them and then choose Stacks > Group as Stack. The number of images in the stack appears in the upper-left corner of the stack thumbnail.

Figure 3.9 *Stacking images keeps them tidy, but accessible.*

- To expand the stack and view all of the images in it, select it and choose Stacks > Open Stack.

- To collapse the stack so that only the top thumbnail is visible, select it and choose Stacks > Close Stack.

4

Laying the Foundation

You'll accomplish your image-editing goals much more quickly—and with less frustration—if you take a little time to get to know some of the basic concepts involved. For example, many techniques require you to make selections or work with layers.

Some of the things covered in this chapter are available only in Full Edit mode (such as tabbed documents or the Layers panel), but others are of use in two or three modes. I'll let you know in each section where the concept is relevant.

Opening files

No matter which mode you're using—Quick Fix, Guided Edit, or Full Edit—you need to open an image in Photoshop Elements to make the edits.

If you know where to find the photo you want to work with, choose File > Open, navigate to the folder that holds your photo, select the image file (or multiple files in the same folder), and click Open.

If you're not sure where the photo is, or even which one you want to work with, use the Organizer (Windows) or Bridge (Mac OS) to find it.

In the Organizer, select the image or images (Ctrl-click to select more than one), and then choose Edit > Edit With Photoshop Elements. Or, if you know which mode you want to use, select the image or images, click the arrow next to the Fix tab, and choose Full Photo Edit, Quick Photo Edit, or Guided Photo Edit to open the photos in the Editor in that mode. (You can change modes once the images are open in the Editor.)

Figure 4.1 *Use the Fix tab menu in the Organizer to open an image in the Editor.*

In Windows, you can also drag images from the Organizer (or anywhere else on your hard drive or a removable drive) into the Project Bin at the bottom of the Editor window.

In Bridge, select the image or images (Command-click to select more than one) and then choose File > Open With > Adobe Photoshop Elements 8.0.

note **If you need to import images from a camera, CD, or other device onto your hard drive, see Chapter 1.**

Camera Raw files

Some cameras can save images in a native raw file format, which is often preferable to other formats. You gain flexibility by saving in raw format, because settings such as white balance, tonal range, and sharpness aren't "baked" into raw files the way they are in JPEG, TIFF, or PNG images.

Raw images have file formats such as NEF and CRW, depending on the type of camera you have. Photoshop Elements supports many camera raw formats. Visit Adobe.com to see whether yours is on the list, or you could just take a couple of trial shots and see whether Photoshop Elements recognizes them.

When you open a raw file, Photoshop Elements opens the Camera Raw dialog box, which gives you numerous processing features. To learn more about working with raw images, see Photoshop Elements help.

Choosing an image mode

Most of the time, you'll want to work in RGB mode in Photoshop Elements. RGB stands for red, green, blue. Together, those three colors can make up a vast and flexible range of colors. However, there are other image modes available in Photoshop Elements.

To change the image mode, choose Image > Mode > [image mode]. Always make a copy of the image file before converting the image mode, so that you can return to it and make changes if necessary.

- For most images, work in RGB mode.

- If you're working with only black and white data, choose Bitmap mode.

- If you're working with black-and-white images that include grays, choose Grayscale mode.

- If you're saving the image in GIF or PNG 8 format, convert it to Indexed Color mode. Because Indexed Color mode significantly limits the colors available, work in RGB mode as long as possible.

Saving files

It's good practice to save files frequently. In fact, I recommend saving a copy of the image as soon as you open it in Photoshop Elements. If you work on a copy, you can experiment without worrying about damaging your original. To save a copy, choose File > Save As. Name the file and select a location for it.

When you make your working copy, save it as a PSD (Photoshop) file so that you won't lose any image data. Your digital camera may save photos in JPEG format, but it's better to use the PSD format rather than resave a photo in JPEG format unless you are ready to share it or use it on a web page. Each time you save in JPEG format, the image data is compressed, potentially causing some data to be lost. You may start to notice reduced image quality after saving the file as a JPEG two or three times. The disadvantage of saving in PSD format is that the file size will increase significantly because the file is not compressed.

Photoshop Elements can save images in several file formats. Which one you use depends on how you plan to use the image. If you are working with web images, the Save For Web command provides many options for optimizing images. If you need to convert several images to the same file format or the same size and resolution, use the Process Multiple Files command.

tip You can set your preferences to automatically open the Save As dialog box the first time you save a file. To do so, choose Edit > Preferences > Saving Files (Windows) or Photoshop Elements > Preferences > Saving Files (Mac OS). Then, choose Always Ask from the On First Save menu.

The Photoshop Elements workspace

Take a look around the Photoshop Elements workspace. In the middle is the image window, where you actually edit your photo. On the left is a toolbox; which tools are available depends on which edit mode you're in. Across the top are the menu bar, the Application bar, and the options bar. The menu bar is the place to go for most of the program's commands. The Application bar has handy shortcuts to the Organizer or Bridge and to common tasks, such as Undo and Redo. The options bar displays the options for the tool that is currently selected. For example, when the Zoom tool is selected, the options bar displays options for resizing the window.

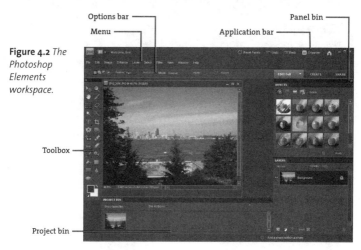

Figure 4.2 *The Photoshop Elements workspace.*

Panels

Panels, such as the Layers panel or the Undo History panel, help you manage and edit images. They often have menus with additional commands and options. To open a panel, choose Window > [panel name].

What's in your toolbox?

Photoshop Elements includes tools for selecting, editing, and viewing images and parts of an image. In Quick Fix and Guided Edits modes, you have a smaller selection of tools than are available in Full Edit mode.

To use a tool, select it in the toolbox. If the tool is part of a group, it may be hidden. To find it, click the visible tool in its group and then choose the one you want to use from the pop-up menu. (A small triangle indicates the tool is part of a tool group.)

When a tool is selected, its options appear in the options bar.

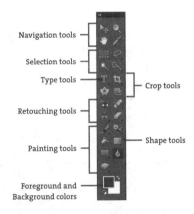

Figure 4.3 *In Full Edit mode, the toolbox is extensive. You can change it from one column to two, or vice versa, by clicking the double arrows at the top of the toolbox.*

Navigation tools
Selection tools
Type tools
Crop tools
Retouching tools
Shape tools
Painting tools
Foreground and Background colors

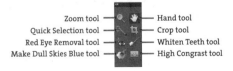

Figure 4.4 *The toolbox in Quick Edit mode contains just a few touch-up and selection tools.*

Zoom tool — Hand tool
Quick Selection tool — Crop tool
Red Eye Removal tool — Whiten Teeth tool
Make Dull Skies Blue tool — High Congrast tool

The panel bin is the default location for any open panels. You can leave panels in the bin, or you can drag a panel's tab outside the panel to work with it independently. To group panels together, drag the tab of one next to the tab of another.

tip To get file information or positioning data for an image, open the Info panel and move your pointer over the image. The Info panel reports color data, x- and y-coordinates, width and height, and the angle of rotation or skewing.

The Project Bin

At the bottom of the Photoshop Elements window is the Project Bin, which displays thumbnails of your open files.

- To switch between images, just double-click the thumbnail of the one you want to work with. They all stay open until you close them, but only one image is active at a time. (Okay, that's not completely true. When you perform some tasks, such as using the Photomerge features, more than one image may be active.)

- To close an image, whether it's active in the image window or not, right-click or Control-click its thumbnail in the Project Bin and choose Close.

- To view information about an image file, right-click or Control-click its thumbnail, and choose File Info.

- To duplicate an image, right-click or Control-click its thumbnail, choose Duplicate, and then name the copy of the file.

- To rotate an image, right-click or Control-click its thumbnail, and choose Rotate 90° Left or Rotate 90° Right.

- To see the filenames of all the open images, right-click or Control-click in the Project Bin, and then choose Show Filenames.

Figure 4.5 *All your open images are shown in the Project Bin.*

Tabbed documents

If you have more than one image open in Full Edit mode, you can arrange them as tabbed documents, so that each image has a tab labeled with its file name. To switch to a different image, click its tab.

- To dock a floating document as a tabbed document, drag its title bar up until a blue line appears at the top of the image window, and then drop it.

- To quickly make all images tabbed, choose Window > Images > Consolidate All To Tabs.

- To release tabbed documents, choose Window > Images > Float All In Windows. Photoshop Elements floats each image window separately, so you can resize and reposition each.

Figure 4.6 *Tabbed documents are tidy, but still accessible.*

note To view all of the open images at the same time, choose a layout option from the Arrange pop-up menu on the options bar. You can tile image windows vertically, horizontally, or in other configurations.

Rulers and the grid

If you're aiming for precision, you may find the rulers and grid handy. Choose View > Rulers to display rulers around the image. You can pull nonprinting ruler guides out from either the vertical or horizontal ruler to help you line things up just right. Choose View > Grid to display a grid on your image.

note Rulers and the grid appear only over the selected image. You need to apply them separately to each image you want to use them with.

Previewing changes

In Guided Edit mode or Quick Fix mode, you can see your original photo next to the edited version as you work. In Quick Fix mode, choose an option from the View menu that appears below the image window. In Guided Edit mode, select a Guided Edit, and then click at the bottom of the panel to choose After Only, Before And After Vertical, or Before And After Horizontal.

To see before and after views in Full Edit mode, duplicate the image in the Project Bin and then choose an option from the Arrange menu to see them side by side as you make edits to one. Just remember which one you're editing and which one you're leaving as the original! You may want to name the duplicate something like "original" or even "don't change this one!"

Undoing actions

Half the fun of editing images is in experimenting, and sometimes experiments don't turn out so well. As with most applications, Photoshop Elements includes an Undo function. I recommend you get mighty familiar with it. In fact, this is one place that it's a great idea to learn the keyboard shortcut.

To undo the last thing you did, choose Edit > Undo. Or press Ctrl+Z (Window) or Command+Z (Mac OS). You can continue to undo multiple actions.

The Undo History panel keeps track of your actions. You can go backward to any point in time, immediately undoing all the changes you've made since that moment; just click the point you want to return to. The actions you've undone are only dimmed—so if you want to restore them, just scroll down the Undo History panel to a more recent point.

Figure 4.7 *Move back through time using the Undo History panel.*

To open the Undo History panel, choose Window > Undo History.

note The Undo History panel is available only in Full Edit mode.

Changing foreground and background colors

See those swatches at the bottom of the toolbox? They determine the foreground (top) and background (bottom) colors at any point in time. Most of the painting tools, including the Brush and Pencil tools, paint in the foreground color. The Eraser tool replaces existing pixels with the background color. Many other tools and features use the foreground and background colors, too, so you should check them frequently and get comfortable changing them.

- To change the foreground or background color, click its swatch and then select a new color from the Color Picker.

- To change the foreground or background color to a color you already have in your image, click the swatch. The cursor becomes an eyedropper that you can use to sample a color in the image.

- To set the foreground and background boxes to black and white, click the Default Colors icon.

- To switch the colors in the two boxes, click the Switch Colors icon.

Figure 4.8

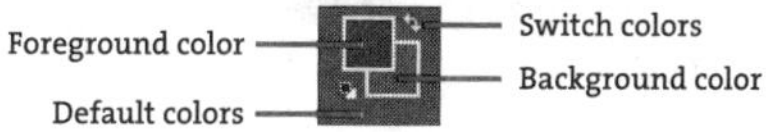

Foreground color ———   ——— Switch colors
                                ——— Background color
Default colors ———

Working with selections

Some changes, like cropping or adjusting the image resolution, apply to an entire photo. But others are best applied to only a portion of the image. For example, you might want to change the color of a specific object, or lighten just the background. To modify only part of a photo, you need to make a *selection*. You can make selections in Full Edit and Quick Fix modes, but not in Guided Edit mode.

note When you have made a selection, only the area within that selection is editable. You can't do anything to the areas outside the selection until you deselect it.

Selections appear on the screen with an active border that is sometimes referred to as "marching ants." You can hide the selection border by choosing View > Selection. But don't forget it's there!

Selection tools

In Quick Fix mode, you're limited to the Quick Selection tool. But in Full Edit mode, there's a full range of selection tools available to you. Which tool you use depends on what you're trying to select and how complex the image is.

The Rectangular Marquee and Elliptical Marquee tools draw rectangular or elliptical selections.

Figure 4.9 *The Rectangular Marquee and Elliptical Marquee tools.*

The Lasso tool draws freehand selections. It has two variants: The Polygonal Lasso tool draws straight segments as you click a selection. The Magnetic Lasso tool guesses the area you're attempting to select and automatically snaps to the edges as you drag the cursor over them.

Figure 4.10 *The Lasso tools.*

The Magic Wand tool really does seem magical sometimes. With it, you can select all the pixels of a similar color with a single click.

Figure 4.11 *The Magic Wand tool.*

The Quick Selection tool makes a selection based on both color and texture when you click or keep the mouse down as you drag over an area. It can be a little sloppy, so you might have to refine the selection—but it *is* quick, as advertised.

The Selection Brush tool selects the area you paint. If you're in Mask mode, it deselects that area, leaving the rest of the photo selected.

Figure 4.12 *The Quick Selection and Selection Brush tools.*

Making selections

To make a selection, use one of the tools to create a selection border around the area you want to select.

Figure 4.13 *Selection borders appear as moving dotted lines.*

To deselect a selection, choose Select > Deselect.

 Selections are limited to the active layer.

To delete a selection, choose Edit > Delete, press the Backspace or Delete key, or choose Edit > Cut. (If you choose Edit > Cut, the selection is copied to the clipboard and you can paste it someplace else.)

If you delete a selection on the Background layer, that area is replaced by the background color. To make the area transparent, you must first convert the Background layer to a regular layer by renaming it. Photoshop Elements indicates transparency with a checkerboard pattern.

If you want to select all the pixels on a layer, select the layer in the Layers panel and choose Select > All.

Fine-tuning selection borders

Your first shot at a selection may not do the trick. You can add to or subtract from a selection using the same tool—or a different selection tool. Just select the appropriate option in the selection bar before you use the selection tool. The options look different depending on the tool you're using. Most show rectangles adding to or being removed from a selection. The Quick Selection tool displays with a plus sign or minus sign next to them.

Figures 4.14-4.15
Select an icon from the options bar to add to or subtract from a selection as you use a selection tool.

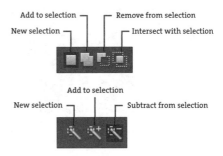

- To expand or contract a selection by a specific number of pixels, choose Select > Modify > Expand or Contract. Then specify by how many pixels you want to expand or contract the selection, and click OK.

- To select only the outline of the selection, choose Select > Modify > Border. Then enter a value between 1 and 200 pixels for the width of the border, and click OK. Photoshop Elements modifies the selection to include only the pixels in the soft-edged border you've created.

- To select stray bits of color, such as hair, when you've used the Magic Wand tool or another color-based selection method, choose Select > Modify > Smooth. Then enter a sample radius between 1 and 100 (depending on how far outside the selection you want Photoshop Elements to look for matching pixels), and click OK.

- To smooth the edges of a selection, select Anti-Aliased in the options bar before you make the selection. Anti-aliasing softens the transition between pixels on the edge of the selection and background pixels. Only the edge pixels change, so you don't lose any detail.

tip **To apply feathering, enter a feather value in the options bar before you make the selection. To add feathering to an existing selection, choose Select > Feather, select a value for the feather radius, and click OK. Feathering smoothes the edges of a selection by blurring them, so you may lose some detail at the edge of the selection.**

Defringing a selection

If there are extra pixels around a selection, creating a halo effect, defringe the selection. To defringe a selection:

1. Copy and paste the selection into a new or existing layer.

2. Choose Enhance > Adjust Color > Defringe Layer.

3. Specify how many pixels you want to replace around the selection. Typically 1 or 2 is fine.

4. Click OK.

When you defringe a layer, Photoshop Elements replaces the color of fringe pixels with the colors of nearby pixels that don't contain any background color.

Inverting a selection

You can swap the selected area with the nonselected areas, inverting the selection. This can be very handy if the area you want to select is complex, but it's on a simple background. Select the background first, and then invert the selection.

To invert a selection, choose Select > Inverse.

Figures 4.16-4.17
Sometimes it's easiest to select what you don't want, and then invert the selection.

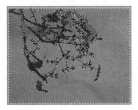 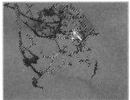

Moving a selection

You can move a selection elsewhere in the image or to a different photo.

1. With a selection tool active, select the Move tool.

2. Drag the selection to a new position. You can also nudge it a pixel at a time using the arrow keys on your keyboard. (Press Shift as you use the arrow keys to move the selection 10 pixels at a time.)

tip   If you just want to remove the selected area from the photo, you don't need to move it. Just press the Delete key to fill the area with transparency or, on a Background layer, with the current background color.

Figure 4.18 *When you move a selection, the content within the selection moves with it, leaving behind transparency or the background color.*

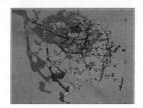

Copying selections

You can also copy a selection without moving it. Probably the easiest way is just to choose Edit > Copy, and then go where you want to copy the selection and choose Edit > Paste. When you cut or copy a selection, it's stored in the clipboard; only one selection can be in the clipboard at a time.

> **tip** Choosing Edit > Copy selects only the pixels in the active layer. Choose Edit > Copy Merged to copy all the layers in the selected area. You can also copy selections between photos by pressing Alt or Option as you use the Move tool.

Selections keep their original pixel dimensions when you copy. If you paste a selection into a photo that has a different resolution, the pasted area may appear out of proportion with the rest of the image. To avoid headaches, make sure the source and destination photos have the same resolution before copying and pasting. (Choose Image > Resize > Image Size, and then change the image resolution if necessary.)

Saving a selection

For more complicated procedures, you may want to save a selection to use again later. To save a selection, choose Select > Save Selection. Then choose New from the pop-up menu, name the selection, and click OK.

To load a selection you've saved, choose Select > Load Selection, select the one you want to use, and then click OK.

Working with layers

Layers offer flexibility and all sorts of creative possibilities. They also provide a sort of safety net, making it possible to work on individual aspects of an image without permanently changing the original, under-lying image. You can use layers to add shapes, apply effects, change the opacity, modify the color and brightness, add new backgrounds, and just about anything else you want to do.

Every image has at least one layer. When you first open an image in Photoshop Elements, it creates a Background layer for the image. In addi-tion to the layers you add yourself, Photoshop Elements creates layers when you perform certain tasks, including many of the Quick Fixes. Photoshop Elements also creates a separate layer when you add text or a shape to your image.

To keep your layers under control, make friends with the Layers panel. There, you can select which layer you want to work on, rearrange the order of layers, and even create web animations using layers. If the Layers panel isn't already open, choose Window > Layers to display it.

Figure 4.19 *The Layers panel.*

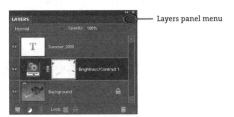

Layers panel menu

note The Layers panel is available only in Full Edit mode.

Layers appear in the image in the order they're listed in the Layers panel. The top layer in the panel is the top layer in the image. Where there is no content in a layer, you can see through it to the layers below. You can change how the layers interact with each other by changing the opacity and applying blending modes.

Creating layers

The Background layer is automatically there when you open the image. To create a new blank layer, click the New Layer icon at the bottom of the Layers panel. To name it, double-click the name in the Layers panel and type a new name.

> **tip** If you want to name a layer as you create it, choose Layer > New > Layer. You'll see a dialog box that lets you name the layer and set options for it as you create it.

A new layer is added above the selected layer in the Layers panel.

About that Background layer

The Background layer that Photoshop Elements automatically creates for your original image is always the bottom layer. Because the Background layer contains the original image data, it's locked. But sometimes you want to move it in the stacking order, change its blending mode, or modify its opacity. To do any of these things, you must first convert it to a regular layer so it's no longer locked.

To convert the Background layer to a regular layer, double-click it and name it anything but Background. Note that the New Layer dialog box appears, but you're actually renaming the Background layer.

If you just want to copy the Background layer, but leave the original in place, select the layer and choose Duplicate Layer from the Layers panel menu.

You can copy a selection onto a new layer, too. Make the selection and then choose Layer > New > Layer Via Copy. (If you want to remove the selection from the original image, choose Layer > New > Layer Via Cut.) Photoshop Elements creates a new layer that contains only the selection, in its original position.

Modifying and arranging layers

Once a layer exists, you can select it, show it, hide it, change its position in the stacking order, lock it, copy it, or reposition it. You can also merge layers or simplify them. You cannot, however, fold, spindle, or mutilate layers in Photoshop Elements (unless you're far more creative than I am).

- To select a layer, click it in the Layers panel. The selected layer is highlighted so you can see which layer is active. Changes you make affect only the active layer.

- To hide a layer, click the eye icon next to it.

- To make a layer visible, click the box so that the eye icon appears.

- To lock all of a layer's properties, select it and then click the Lock All button at the bottom of the Layers panel.

- To lock only the transparent areas of a layer, ensuring that no painting affects them, click the Lock Transparent Pixels icon at the bottom of the Layers panel.

> **note** Transparency is always locked for text and shape layers. To unlock it, you must first simplify the layer.

- To simplify a complex layer, such as a type, shape, or gradient layer, select it and choose Layer > Simplify. You must simplify complex layers before you can apply filters to them or edit them. Note, though, that after you've simplified a layer, you can no longer use the type- or shape-editing options on them.

- To delete a layer, select it in the Layers panel and click the Delete icon at the bottom of the panel.

- To copy a layer to another image, open both images and then drag the layer name from the source image onto the other image window.

Figures 4.20-4.21
To copy a layer to another image, just drag it from the Layers panel.

- To reposition the contents of a layer in the image, select the contents with the Move tool and then slide the layer where you want it. You can also scale a layer or otherwise transform it.

- To change the order of layers in the Layers panel, drag them into their new positions.

- To merge layers into a single layer, select them and choose Merge Layers from the Layers panel menu. If you want to merge all layers into a single layer, choose Layer > Flatten Image. When you merge layers, any that aren't currently visible are discarded. Keep in mind that once you've merged layers, you cannot return to the individual layers to edit them.

Opacity and blending modes

At first, no pixels are transparent in an image or in a new layer you create. But you can change that by adjusting the Opacity value.

To change the opacity of a layer, select the layer and then change the Opacity value at the top of the Layers panel.

> **note** You can't change the opacity of a Background layer while it's a Background layer. But you can change it if you convert the layer to a regular layer. To convert it, double-click it and rename it anything but Background.

Blending modes are similar to opacity—and, in fact, use transparency—in that they determine how the pixels in one layer interact with the pixels in the layers beneath it. Blending modes are a great way to get creative with an image.

> **note** You can also set opacity and blending modes for painting tools. The opacity and blending modes set for the layer interact with the settings for the tool.

By default, the Normal blending mode is applied to a layer. To change the blending mode, select the layer and then choose an option from the Blending Mode menu at the top of the Layers panel.

> **tip** In Windows, you can preview blending modes quickly. Choose one, and then press the up or down arrow keys on your keyboard to scroll through the options.

> **note** For more information about blending modes, see the sidebar "Blend Away" on pages 83–85.

Figure 4.22 *Change the opacity and blending mode to combine layers in interesting ways.*

Fill and adjustment layers

Fill layers create an entire layer with a solid color, gradient, or pattern fill. Fill layers don't affect the layers below them, but you can't paint on a fill layer unless you simplify it.

Adjustment layers give you the freedom to edit and re-edit lighting, levels, and other color and tonal changes. By default, an adjustment layer affects all the layers below it. You can hide adjustment layers, revealing the original image below. Chapter 8 covers adjustment layers in detail, but you'll use them if you work with Quick Fixes, as well.

To add a fill layer or an adjustment layer, click the Create New Fill Or Adjustment Layer button at the bottom of the Layers panel. Then, choose the kind of layer you want to create.

Figure 4.23 *Click the Create New Fill Layer Or Adjustment Layer button to add a fill layer or adjustment layer.*

Layer styles

Just as paragraph styles in a word-processing application let you apply multiple attributes to text at once, layer styles apply multiple effects to a layer. To see the predefined layer styles, click the Layer Styles button at the top of the Effects panel. To use one, select a style type from the menu, select a style, and click Apply.

Figure 4.24 *Select a layer style type to see the available layer styles.*

The layer style is applied to the entire layer; if you edit the layer, effects in the layer style are updated, too. For example, if you apply a drop shadow layer style, anything you add to the layer will automatically have a drop shadow, as well. Likewise, if you move the layer, the effects move with it.

Layer styles are cumulative, so you can create a complex effect by applying multiple styles to a layer. An fx icon appears next to the layer when a layer style or other effect has been applied.

To remove a layer style, select the layer and then choose Layer > Layer Style > Clear Layer Style.

Blend away!

Mundane photo? Not sure what to try next? Blending modes to the rescue! They change the way layers play together. Some intensify color while others replace it. Some adjust contrast or lighting. Mainly, they're a lot of fun. Start with an image, add a pattern layer, and then try out blending modes to see what you get. In these examples, I started with a photo of a tree with orange fall leaves, added a layer of a simple pattern from the Effects panel, and then just let the blending modes do their thing. The differences are more obvious in color, of course, but you can see them even in black and white.

There are essentially six categories of blending modes.

The Normal Modes are Normal and Dissolve. Normal hides pixels unless the top layer has transparency. Dissolve randomly replaces pixels with the color of either layer, so the top layer appears to dissolve into the one beneath it. Pretty cool.

The Darkening modes result in a darker image. Darken, Multiply, Color Burn, Linear Burn, and Darker Color all darken in different ways.

Figure 4.25
Linear Burn.

The Lightening modes always result in a lighter image. Lighten, Screen, Color Dodge, Linear Dodge, and Lighter Color lighten different parts of the image.

(continued on next page)

Blend away (continued)

Figure 4.26
Color Dodge.

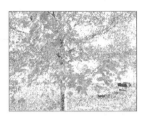

The Overlay modes result in greater contrast. Overlay, Soft Light, Hard Light, Vivid Light, Linear Light, Pin Light, and Hard Mix produce interesting and varied appearances.

Figure 4.27
Linear Light.

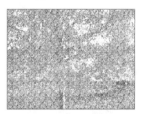

The Difference modes compare the colors in the layers with each other. Difference creates greater contrast, and Exclusion results in lower contrast.

Figure 4.28
Exclusion.

Blend away (continued)

The Hue modes affect the actual color values. Hue, Saturation, Color, and Luminosity each affect the respective attribute of the image.

Figure 4.29 *Hue.*

Managing color

Have you ever printed a photo and noticed that it looked different on paper than it did on your computer? That's because different devices (digital cameras, computer monitors, scanners, printers) can portray different ranges of colors. If you're not managing those colors, the translation from computer monitor to printer can produce surprising, and often disappointing, results.

Color management systems map colors from one device to another, so that what you see on your computer monitor more closely approximates what you'll get when you print. Of course, if you're posting your files to the web, this isn't such a big issue. But if you plan to print the photos you're editing, take a few minutes to set up color management so that your edits will help you get the best printed results.

To manage color for your images, choose Edit > Color Settings. Then, choose either Always Optimize Colors For Computer Screens, Always Optimize For Printing, or Allow Me To Choose. Click OK.

Photoshop Elements uses color profiles (called ICC profiles) to manage color. The option you choose determines which profile the application uses to interpret and display colors. You don't have to know much about color management to use it in Photoshop Elements. Just select the option that makes sense for the way you use photos. If almost all of your images are bound for the web, optimize for the screen. If almost all are destined to be printed, optimize for printing. And if you do some of each, opt to choose.

Quick Fixes

You can dramatically improve most photos with a simple click or two, using the Quick Fix options in Photoshop Elements. If you're just trying to lighten up an image, remove red eye, or ditch a color cast, start with Quick Fix options. If they don't quite do it, you can always continue to tinker with the image in Full Edit mode.

To enter Quick Fix mode, choose Edit Quick from the pop-up menu at the top of the screen. Quick Fix mode includes a few special tools, such as the Red Eye Removal, Whiten Teeth, and High Contrast tools. However, most of the Quick Fix options are in the Quick Fix panel on the right of the screen.

Figure 5.1 *Choose Edit Quick from the pop-up menu.*

I recommend viewing both the Before and After versions as you work, so you can see how the changes affect your photo. To see both, choose Before & After – Horizontal or Before & After – Vertical from the View menu at the bottom of the image window.

Changes you apply using the Quick Fix tools and settings appear in the After image; the Before image is locked until you accept your changes. To accept the changes, click the Commit (check mark) button next to the quick fix category name.

Previewing quick fixes

One of the benefits of using a quick fix is the opportunity to preview settings quickly. Any quick fix option with a slider includes a grid icon; click the icon to display preview thumbnails for different settings. The current setting has a yellow arrow on its thumbnail. As you move the cursor over the preview options, the After image changes so you can see how your photo will look if you apply that setting. If you select one of the preview options, click the check mark that appears next to the quick fix section to accept the change—or the X to cancel it.

Figure 5.2 *Click the grid to preview thumbnails of different settings.*

Making cosmetic adjustments

The quick fix tools give you quick ways to remove red eye, brighten a smile, intensify a blue sky, and create high-contrast areas in an image. The tools are pretty easy to use, once you know how they work.

Removing red eye

My nephew can be a little mischievous, but he's no demon. Still, when I snap a flash photo, light reflects off the retinas in his eyes, and he ends up looking a bit evil.

You can quickly exorcise such demons in Photoshop Elements. In Quick Fix mode, zoom into your photo so you can see the eyes clearly. Then, select the Red Eye Removal tool.

You can adjust the pupil size and darkening percentage, but for most photos, the defaults are fine. Just drag the Red Eye Removal tool around the eye, and release the mouse. Presto! The eye is human again.

Figure 5.3 *Drag the Red Eye Removal tool around the eye.*

tip The same trick works for red eye in pets, but you may need to tweak the pupil size a little.

Brightening a smile

It won't replace a trip to the dentist, but the Whiten Teeth tool in Photoshop Elements can make dull teeth brighter.

Zoom in to the area you want to whiten, and then select the Whiten Teeth tool. I find I usually need to make the brush smaller, using the settings in the options bar.

Drag a selection over the area you want to brighten. Be careful not to include the gums or lips, as you can end up with some clownish results. If you accidentally select an area you shouldn't have, click the Subtract From Selection button in the options bar and then click the areas you want to remove. You can go back and forth using the add and delete brushes until you've got the area you want. You may want to zoom in and out to get a feel for the effect. To preview the teeth without seeing the selection, click the Hand tool.

Photoshop Elements makes all the changes on a separate adjustments layer called Pearly Whites, so you can hide it in Full Edit mode if you don't like the effect.

Deepening a blue sky

Sometimes pictures lie. A rich blue sky may be washed out because of lighting, angle, or reflections. You can put the blue back in that sky using the Make Dull Skies Blue tool.

Select the tool, and then brush in the selection for the sky. If you overselect, use the Subtract From Selection brush to scale it back.

That's all there is to it. Now, that's a quick fix!

 Unfortunately, this tool doesn't turn a white sky blue. It intensifies the blue that's already there.

Figure 5.4
Select the sky with the Make Dull Skies Blue tool to deepen the color.

Photoshop Elements creates an adjustment layer called Blue Skies, so you can continue to tweak it or turn it on and off in Full Edit mode.

tip You can get cool results using this tool over other colors, too. Photoshop Elements applies a blue layer with a color burn blending mode and 75% opacity to the area you select.

Converting areas to high-contrast black and white

The High Contrast tool is practical, but it's also a lot of fun. This tool simulates the effect you'd get if you used a red filter lens on a camera while shooting with black and white film.

You can use this tool to convert your photo to high-contrast black and white. That can be very useful if, for example, you're sending an image to the local newspaper and want to make sure it will print well.

So how does this get fun? Drag a selection over just part of your image to turn it into high-contrast black and white. You can make the background black and white, leaving your subject in color, or vice versa. Or convert everything to black and white except a single red rose. Or—and now you see how this can get very creative—leave the entire scene in color except the TV screen. Poof! Instant black-and-white television show.

You're not actually losing the color in the shot. Photoshop Elements puts these changes on an adjustment layer called High Contrast Red Filter, so you can get back to your full-color photo any time you want to.

Adjusting lighting and color

You can get very fussy with both lighting and color in Full Edit mode, but even Quick Fix mode gives you a fair amount of control. To fix both lighting and color quickly, try Smart Fix. Otherwise, play around with the lighting and color options to see what you can do.

Applying Smart Fix

For overall improvements to an image, try Smart Fix. It's the first of the options in the Quick Fix panel. Smart Fix adjusts both lighting and color, and it can also improve shadow and highlight detail.

Click Auto to see what Photoshop Elements recommends. Or select one of the preview options. You can nudge the slider slightly by clicking and dragging on the preview option itself. You can also just drag the Smart Fix slider, of course.

Figure 5.5 *Adjust lighting and color quickly.*

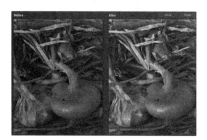

Changing the lighting

For a quick fix, the Lighting section on the panel gives you quite a bit of control. You can adjust the overall contrast of an image, lighten shadows, darken highlights, and adjust the contrast in the midtones.

Figure 5.6 *Some quick fixes adjust only the lighting.*

We'll start from the top. Levels, which determine tonal levels, are pretty sophisticated, and Chapter 8 covers them in more depth. However, in the Quick Fix panel, you have only the Auto option, so you'll either like the results or you won't.

Click it and give it a try. The Levels option individually maps the lightest and darkest pixels in each color channel to black and white. It may affect the color of the image, which can be very useful if you want to remove a color cast.

Contrast is a little more clear-cut, and I mean that literally. This option makes highlights lighter and shadows darker. Click Auto next to Contrast when the colors are right but the photo needs more contrast.

Now you're back to having a little more control. Lighten Shadows, Darken Highlights, and Midtone Contrast each include sliders and preview options. You can move the slider yourself, or use the preview thumbnails to see the effect of different settings.

Each of these options does just what it says. Lightening shadows brings out details without affecting the highlights (and has no effect on pure black areas of the image.) Darkening highlights gives depth to the lightest areas of the image (and has no effect on pure white areas). And Midtone Contrast takes care of everything in between—adjusting the contrast within the values that are in the middle of the spectrum.

Tweaking color

If the reds aren't red enough—or should be yellow—use the Color options. The overall Color option adjusts both contrast and color; click Auto to apply it. You may see the Saturation or Hue slider move, or possibly both!

Figure 5.7 *You can adjust Saturation and Hue.*

Saturation determines how vivid the colors are. Check out the preview options to see just how extreme you can get. Then move the slider where you want it.

Hue affects the color itself. You can quickly go from a fairly natural scene to one that might appear more fantasy-like. In fact, the changes are so dramatic that it's probably best to keep the changes small. Remember that you can make a selection to affect only that area of the image.

Fine-tuning color balance

There's yet another way to affect the color. You can adjust the color balance to make the colors warmer or cooler, or to remove (or add) a color cast.

Figure 5.8 *You can adjust the temperature and tint, as well.*

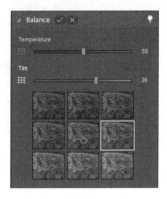

The Temperature settings make the colors redder (warmer) or bluer (cooler). Experiment with the preview options. Sometimes, you may not even realize the image is slightly off until you see how much a subtle change in temperature improves it.

Tint makes colors more green or more magenta. You can get some pretty freaky results, and if you're feeling creative, that may be your goal. But for most purposes, you'll only want to use this option to fine-tune the colors after adjusting the color temperature.

Enhancing detail

If you want to sharpen your image, move the Sharpen slider or check out the preview options. This feature only sharpens; you cannot use it to blur images. The slider begins all the way to the left.

Click Auto to apply the default amount of sharpening, but be prepared to undo if you don't like the effect.

Figure 5.9
Sharpen an image to bring out the detail.

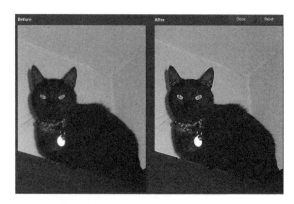

> **tip** Because even a small amount of sharpening can dramatically change the look of an image, double-click the Zoom tool to zoom to 100% before sharpening so you can see how the image will look as you intend to use it.

Making quick adjustments in Organizer

If you're using Photoshop Elements for Windows, you can access several quick fix options within Organizer. As you browse your images, you can fix red eye or change the lighting without ever having to go into the Editor.

In Organizer, click the Fix tab. (Make sure to click the tab—if you select the menu, you'll see options that take you into Editor.)

Figure 5.10 *You can make some quick fixes in the Organizer.*

Select the photo or photos you want to fix, and then click the appropriate button. For example, to fix red eye, click Auto Red Eye Fix.

There are no sliders or preview options in the Organizer, only auto options. Still, for many photos, auto Color, Smart Fix, Levels, Sharpen, Contrast, and Red Eye Fix can do the job nicely and quickly.

To crop a photo, select it and then click Crop. Resize the crop box and move it to the area you want to keep. Click the check mark to accept the change, or the X to cancel it. Then, click OK in the Crop Options dialog box.

Photoshop Elements displays a progress bar as it makes the change you request, and then groups the edited photo with the original in a version set. To see all the images in a version set, right-click the thumbnail and choose Version Set > Expand Items In Version Set.

 To undo any quick changes you make in the Organizer, choose Edit > Undo [fix].

You can also rotate images in Organizer, so that Aunt Martha isn't tipped on her side. Just select the image thumbnail, and then choose Edit > Rotate 90° Left or Rotate 90° Right.

Editing with a Guide

Sometimes you know what you want to do, but you're not quite sure how to go about it. Depending on your goals, Guided Edit mode may be the best way for you to get there.

Not all the guided edits, as Adobe calls them, include that much guidance. Sometimes you actually have more information using a quick fix to accomplish the same thing. That's true for sharpening and some of the lighting changes. Where guided edits really shine are when you're performing more complex or confusing tasks, such as adjusting levels.

Some of the guided edits include Auto options, so you can see how default changes would affect your photo. Many include sliders, as well, but they do not have the preview options that the quick fixes do.

To switch to Guided Edit mode, choose Edit Guided from the pop-up menu in the Edit tab in the panel bin.

Figure 6.1 *Guided edits range from simple to complex.*

When you apply a guided edit, click Done to accept the changes or Cancel to return to the original settings. As with quick fixes, you can choose whether you see only the After view or both Before and After views as you make your changes. I recommend choosing a view that lets you see both the Before and After versions; the menu appears at the bottom of the Guided Edits panel after you select a guided edit.

Basic editing

The first set of guided edits are quick ways to crop or reposition your image, as well as to apply some pretty simple sharpening. The guided edits provide a little context for the Crop, Recompose, and Straighten tools, so if you're new to the features, it may be worth using the guided edit the first time you do it. For sharpening, you're better off in Quick Fix mode.

Cropping

You can crop a photo in any editing mode in Photoshop Elements, or even in the Organizer (in Windows). But if you'd like an explanation of what you're doing as you crop, use Guided Edit mode.

To crop an image, click Crop in the Guided Edit panel. A crop box appears on the image. You can just drag its corners to resize it. However, if you want to crop the photo to specific proportions, such as a standard 3-by-5-inch photo, select a ratio from the Crop Box Size menu. Click Done when you're satisfied, or click Cancel to remove the crop.

Figure 6.2 *Resize and reposition the crop box.*

tip If you want to crop the photo to a shape other than a rectangle, use the Cookie Cutter tool in Full Edit mode. In Chapter 7, you can see the Cookie Cutter tool in action.

Recomposing

The Recompose feature is one of the coolest new features in Photoshop Elements 8. With it, you can crop an image from within. For example, you can remove extra space between two children but leave everything on either side of them intact.

The Recompose guided edit explains the process well. With the image open in Photoshop Elements, click Recompose in the Guided Edit panel. A box appears around your image. You can just start dragging the handles to resize the image and let Photoshop Elements decide what to keep, what to remove, and what to distort. That may not give you the best results, though. Sometimes people in the photo can start to look like they're reflected in a funhouse mirror.

For more control over what stays and what goes, use the Protect Brush and the Remove Brush at the bottom of the panel. With the Protect Brush selected (as it is by default), paint over anything you definitely want to keep in the photo. If there are areas you absolutely want to remove, paint them with the Remove Brush. You can change the brush size using the slider, and use the Eraser brushes to undo any brush strokes where you were overly enthusiastic.

Then drag the handles in as far as you want. If you're happy with the results, click Done. If not, try painting additional areas to fine-tune the process.

Figures 6.3-6.4 *Paint over the areas you want to keep, and then drag the handles inward to recompose the image.*

Rotating and straightening

You can use the Rotate And/Or Straighten guided edit to rotate a photo or to realign it. Using this guided edit, you can rotate only at 90° angles.

To realign the photo, which basically means rotating it at other than a 90-degree angle, click the Straighten tool and then draw a line through the image at the angle you want its baseline to follow. The image will rotate to the angle of the line. It can be a little tricky, so you may have to click Reset a time or two before you get the results you want. When you're satisfied with the image rotation, click Done.

Figure2 6.5-6.6 *To straighten an image, draw a line at the appropriate angle.*

 After you've straightened an image, you'll probably want to crop it to the canvas.

Sharpening

The Sharpen Photo guided edit includes only the Sharpen slider and an Auto setting. If you're new to sharpening, I recommend using the Sharpen quick fix instead. In addition to the slider and Auto setting, it gives you preview options that let you see how the different settings affect your photo. For more on the Sharpen quick fix, see page 96.

Lighting and color corrections

The Lighten Or Darken guided edit gives you the same sliders for lightening shadows, darkening highlights, and adjusting midtone contrast as the option in Quick Fix mode, but without the previews. However, it also includes an Auto button that isn't available in Quick Fix mode. So if you want to see how Photoshop Elements would adjust these sliders for your image, try Auto.

The Brightness And Contrast guided edit includes two sliders that adjust— you guessed it, the brightness and contrast of the image. Again, there's an Auto button, so you can see how Photoshop Elements would adjust an under-exposed or over-exposed image.

Adjusting levels

The Adjust Levels guided edit really takes advantage of the Guided Edit format. If you're confused about tonal ranges and just what levels are all about, use this guided edit. It walks you through the process of adjusting the black point, white point, and midtones in an image using the Levels dialog box and its histogram. The instructions include helpful diagrams that illustrate what a histogram can tell you about the tonal range.

Best yet, the Adjust Levels guided edit has you create a Levels adjustment layer before you do anything else, so you can feel free to make changes knowing that you are not affecting the underlying image. You can hide or remove the adjustment layer at any time in Full Edit mode—or you can continue to tweak the settings in the Levels dialog box.

Figure 6.7 *The Adjust Levels guided edit provides a great introduction to working with levels.*

Enhancing colors

The Enhance Colors guided edit includes three sliders: Hue, Saturation, and Lightness. If you're only changing the hue or saturation, I'd use the quick fix so you can take advantage of the preview thumbnails. However, if you want to make changes to all three, or are particularly concerned about the lightness, the guided edit is a fine place to work. As with many other guided edits, you can click Auto to see what Photoshop Elements would do to your image, and then either accept that result, fine-tune the settings, or start from scratch with your own settings.

Removing color casts

Removing a color cast is really a one-step procedure, but it's helpful to have the instructions handy, so the Correct Color Cast guided edit is a nice place to start. (Click Remove A Color Cast to get there.)

As the onscreen instructions say, simply use the eyedropper tool to click any place in the photo that should be pure gray, white, or black. Photoshop Elements compares all other colors in the image with the one you select and realigns them, removing an unwanted color cast.

Figure 6.8 *Use the eyedropper to click on a neutral color in order to remove a color cast.*

> **tip** There may not be a perfect place to click in your image. You can click in different places on the image to see how your choices change the overall color, and then select the one that meets your needs.

Correcting skin tones

Color casts often show up in skin tones. If your nephew is looking a little green around the gills but wasn't actually seasick, use the Correct Skin Tone guided edit. This guided edit adjusts the overall color to bring out more natural skin tones. You can adjust the tan (brown), blush (red), and ambient light for the photo.

Click on the skin using the eyedropper tool. Then, adjust the Tan, Blush, and Ambient Light sliders. The entire image is affected, not just the skin, so make sure that while you're correcting skin problems, you aren't creating other issues in your photo.

Guided activities

The guided activities serve as step-by-step guides for editing your photo. If you don't touch up photos very often, or if you want to make sure you're performing steps in a logical order, turn to these guides.

Touching up blemishes

The Touch Up Photo guided edit is most useful if you're working with scanned photos, where the originals might have suffered some wear and tear from years in a shoe box or from an ungraceful exit from a tight picture frame. You can also use this guided edit, though, if you want to apply a bit of cover-up to your daughter's pimple or your own wrinkles.

The Touch Up Photo guided edit uses the Spot Healing Brush tool to repair minor flaws and the Healing Brush tool for those imperfections that aren't so small. If the image has both small and large flaws, use both.

Recommended workflow for editing a photo

The Guide For Editing A Photo guided edit is similar to an editing wizard. It walks you through common editing steps in the order Adobe recommends. When you click Guide For Editing A Photo, the Crop panel opens. Resize the crop box to the area you want to keep. If you don't want to crop the image, be sure to pull the crop box out to the image border; otherwise, Photoshop Elements will crop the image automatically. Click Next when the crop is correct.

The Recompose panel opens next. If you want to crop the image from within, drag the Recompose handles inward. For more precise results, you can use the brushes to paint areas that you want to protect or remove. If you don't want to recompose the image at all, don't do anything. Click Next when the image is recomposed as you want it.

Continue clicking Next as you complete each step: Lighten Or Darken A Photo, Touch Up A Photo, and Sharpen A Photo.

You can perform other editing tasks, but the ones included in this Guided Edit are the most common, and you'll typically have the best results if you edit in a logical sequence. For example, there's no point in correcting a flaw that you're going to crop out of the photo!

Fixing keystone distortion

Keystone distortion refers to the distortion that occurs when the horizontal or vertical lines of a rectangular object are skewed in a photo. This can easily happen if you're tilting the camera up to take a photo of the top of a building, for example.

Figures 6.9-6.10
Before and after keystone distortion is corrected.

The keystone, of course, refers to the point of stability in a building, but skewed lines can occur with any kind of rectangular object.

To correct keystone distortion, use the Correct Camera Distortion dialog box. The guided edit walks you through using this dialog box to correct the distortion. Basically, you use a grid to shift the vertical and horizontal lines into position.

Figure 6.11
Use the grid to see when the building is aligned properly.

After you've adjusted the horizontal and vertical lines, there may be blank areas in the image. You can use the Edge Extension slider to scale the image so that the blank areas don't show.

Photomerge

There are several Photomerge features, and they're all worth getting to know. Each of them lets you combine the best parts of multiple images to create a more ideal composite. You can use these features in Full Edit mode, as well, but putting all the pieces in place may be a little tricky the first few times you do it. Guided edits can help you get good results faster.

Before you select a Photomerge guided edit, open all the images in the Editor and then select them all in the Project Bin.

Photomerge Group Shot

Use this option to combine the best elements from multiple group shots. Say, for example, you got everyone together at the family reunion and took several photos. In one, three people have their eyes closed, but in another, two people were distracted and looking away from the camera. You can use the photo that you consider the better one to be the base, and then replace elements of it with those from the other photo—or up to nine other photos.

First, make sure you've opened the images you want to use and selected them in the Project Bin. Then, click Group Shot. Drag the photo you consider the best—the one you want to use as the base image—from the Project Bin to the Final image box.

For best results, click Advanced Options. Then, take advantage of the Alignment tool and pixel blending. The Alignment tool is a little clunky, in that you need to place three markers in the same position in both the source and base photos—but Photoshop Elements only displays the markers in the active photo. It works best if you choose very distinctive spots for the markers so that Photoshop Elements can find them, and so that you'll remember what you did when you move to the other photo.

Figure 6.12
*Set markers
to align
the photos
for better
results.*

Use the Pencil tool to draw around the areas in the photo on the left that you want to use in the base photo. I recommend selecting Show Regions and Pixel Blending. The regions give you a much better idea of what's going to show up in the final photo than the pencil lines do. Pixel Blending transforms what can be some pretty rough transitions into a smooth, more natural photo.

Photomerge Faces

I haven't found a practical use for this feature yet, but it can be a lot of fun. Photomerge Faces lets you combine facial features from multiple people. It's similar to Photomerge Group Shot in that you start with multiple photos, select a base photo, align it with a source photo, and then identify the parts you want to copy.

You can come up with some delightfully wacky combinations: mustaches on two-year-olds, a Mohawk hair style on your conservative colleague, and so on. There's no Pixel Blending option with this feature, so expect some pretty abrupt changes as the features move from one image to another. As with the group shots, you can pull features from multiple sources, but you can only take from one at a time.

Photomerge Scene Cleaner

If your photo includes airplanes, chipmunks, or little brothers that you'd rather weren't there, this feature is worth a shot. As long as you have two pictures of the area that contains the offending object (one with it, and one without), you may be able to merge the two. Say, for example, you've got a great shot of your brother in the lake but there's a distracting fisherman in the background. If you've got another shot of the lake without your brother or the fisherman, you can combine the two shots for a clean photo.

This can also work well if the object you want to omit was moving across the scene. You can combine multiple images to remove it altogether.

Figure 6.13 *Now you see him.*

Figure 6.14 *Now you don't.*

Photomerge Exposure

Photomerge Exposure combines the best of multiple exposures. If you take one shot with a flash and another without, different parts of the scene are likely to be highlighted in each photo. You can combine the two to see the whole scene. Depending on the images, you may get the best results using the Manual option. This is especially true if you need to align the images—click Advanced Options to get to the Alignment tool.

You can also have some fun with Photomerge Exposure. If you're feeling artsy or philosophical, use it to capture the passage of time. Blending two similar photos in which one or more subjects have moved between the shots can give you some pretty cool results. Use the Automatic option for that effect, unless your images are dramatically misaligned.

Figure 6.15
Photomerge Exposure can illustrate the passage of time.

Action player

Camera, lights, action! Well, not quite. But the Action player is both cool and useful. An action is a series of tasks that Photoshop Elements performs for you with the click of a button. Actions can save you time and the chore of remembering how to achieve a particular goal. Photoshop Elements includes several actions—both creative and practical.

To use actions, click Action Player in the Guided Edits panel. Select an action set, and then the action you want to run. Then, click Play Action.

There are four action sets: Captions, Lose Weight, Resize And Crop, and Special Effects. Captions is a little misleading—it doesn't actually create a caption for you, but a space for a caption. You can select gray, white, or black space added to your image—and then add the caption yourself in Full Edit mode.

While Lose Weight may sound like an order, it's actually an action that slims the subject of your photo. But be aware that this action slims the entire photo, not just an individual. You can choose 2 percent or 4 percent, as many times as you want. The more you "lose weight," of course, the more you distort the photo, so this isn't a good replacement for a sensible diet and sufficient exercise.

Resize And Crop gives you several choices for final image size, and it then crops the image using the center point as a guide.

Don't overlook Special Effects. I'm not sure why they named this category to sound like the CGI in a movie. I'd have named it Nostalgia. My favorite action in this set is the Instant Snapshot, which creates a margin around the photo, with a larger margin at the bottom, like the snapshots of my youth. The Faded Ink and Sepia Toning options may also take you back to the days of well-thumbed photo albums.

Figure 6.16 *You can quickly get sepia effects using actions.*

Photographic effects

The Photographic Effects guided edits walk you through the steps that allow you to transform your photo artistically. You could do all this on your own using the filters in Full Edit mode, but these guided edits are a great way to get used to working with filters and modifying their effects. The Line Drawing guided edit uses the Pencil Sketch filter, and then helps you change the layer opacity and darken the contrast. The Old-Fashioned Photo guided edit uses a filter to convert the image to black and white, and then guides you to adjust tonality, add texture, and adjust the hue and saturation.

Figure 6.17 *The Line Drawing guided edit helps you quickly create an artistic effect for an image.*

The third guided edit in this category is a little different: A single button gives your image a saturated slide film effect, with no additional fine-tuning. It's great if that's the effect you want, but it's not as useful for helping you learn a filter workflow.

7

Common Editing Tasks

In Full Edit mode, you have access to almost everything Photoshop Elements offers: extensive tools, layers, filters, text, and so on. To enter Full Edit mode, choose Edit Full from the Edit pop-up menu.

Some common editing tasks can be completed in Quick Fix or Guided Edit mode. However, many tasks must be done in Full Edit mode. And in Full Edit mode, you have more opportunity to fuss, fiddle, and tweak, even for most of those tasks you could perform in other modes.

Changing image size and resolution

It's not uncommon to need to change the size or resolution of an image for a particular printer or project. And it's easy enough to do. But to get good results, you need to know what you're changing and how it affects other aspects of your photo.

First, a little vocabulary. *Image size* refers to the number of pixels in the width and height of the image. An image size of 3000 pixels wide and 2000 pixels high has a different file size and a different amount of image data than one that is 1500 pixels wide and 1000 pixels high.

Resolution refers to the number of pixels per inch (ppi). More pixels means more detail and higher resolution, which usually means better quality as well.

A digital image contains a fixed amount of image data—once the picture has been taken, you can't add more data to it. But it doesn't have a fixed size or resolution. You can change the resolution of the file, which will also change the physical dimensions of the photo. The inverse is also true, of course: If you change the physical dimensions, the resolution necessarily changes, too.

To see the current dimensions and resolution of an image, choose Document Dimensions from the information menu at the bottom of the image window.

Figure 7.1 *View the photo's dimensions at the bottom of the image window.*

To change the image size or resolution, choose Image > Resize > Image Size. Notice that the pixel dimensions aren't editable. But you can change the width, height, or resolution.

By default, the width, height, and resolution are linked—if you change one, the other two change in relationship to it.

Figure 7.2 *By default, the dimensions and resolution are linked.*

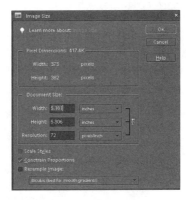

To resample an image, click Resample Image in the Image Size dialog box and then choose a resampling method. The resampling methods are described in the menu and in Photoshop Elements Help. In most cases, you'd want to use either Bicubic Smoother or Bicubic Sharper.

note   Don't resample casually! Resampling requires Photoshop Elements to remove data or to add data (basically making an educated guess about what might have been there)—and it can compromise image fidelity.

Enlarging or shrinking the canvas

The canvas is the workspace within an image window. When you first open an image file, the image usually fills the canvas. But you may want to shrink the canvas size to crop part of the image or expand it to add a border or other objects. To change the canvas size, choose Image > Resize > Canvas Size.

In the Canvas Size dialog box, enter new width and height values for the canvas. Or, if you want to add an even amount of space around the image, select Relative and then type how many inches you want to add to the height and width. To add an inch of extra canvas to each side, type 1 for both width and height. To remove an inch of canvas, type -1. The Anchor determines where the canvas is extended, and it may seem a little unintuitive. By default, the center is selected. If you select the top-center arrow, everything but the top edge will be affected.

Figure 7.3 *You can use relative values to change the canvas size.*

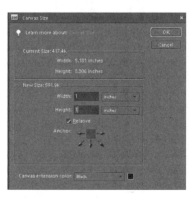

 Some of the Actions in the Action Player guided edit automatically extend the canvas for captions or a snapshot effect.

Cropping an image

There are many reasons to crop a photo: You may want to remove distracting objects, change the focus of the photo, or fit a picture frame. There are also many methods of cropping: You can change the canvas size, use the Crop tool, remove areas within a photo using the Recompose tool, or create an unusual image shape with the Cookie Cutter tool.

Using the Crop tool

The traditional way to crop an image is with the Crop tool. Select it in the toolbox. You can crop an image to any size and it will retain its original resolution. But you can also limit the crop dimensions by entering values for Width and Height or by selecting an aspect ratio in the options bar.

To use the Crop tool, drag it over the area you want to keep. To resize the crop bounding box, drag its corner and side handles. To reposition it, just click and drag it.

Figure 7.4 *Drag the Crop tool over an area to create a crop bounding box.*

tip You can crop the image at an angle! Press Alt or Option as you click outside the crop box, and the cursor turns into a curved arrow. Drag the arrow to rotate the crop box.

When the crop box contains the portion of the photo that you want to keep, click the green Commit button (the check mark) or press Enter or

Return. To cancel the crop, click the red Cancel button in the corner of the crop boundary or press Esc.

Recomposing an image

Until recently, cropping has been limited to removing areas around the outside of a photo. But the Recompose tool changes all that. It can remove sections from any part of an image, not just the outer edges. For example, you can remove extra space between two children playing to keep the focus on them and not the grass between them.

1. Make sure you have a layer selected.

2. Select the Recompose tool. If you haven't used it before, a screen pops up to explain the tool. (To keep that screen from popping up each time, select Don't Show Again in its lower-left corner.) Read the information, and then click OK to close the window.

> **tip** You can just start dragging the edges of the photo in at this point. Photoshop Elements will decide what to keep, what to remove, and what to distort. That may not give you the best results, though. Sometimes people in the photo can start to look like they're reflected in a funhouse mirror.

3. With the Protect Brush selected in the options bar, paint over anything you want to keep in the photo. If there are areas you definitely want to remove, paint them with the Remove Brush. Use the slider if you need to change the brush size, and use the Eraser brushes to undo any brush strokes where you were overly enthusiastic.

> **tip** If you want Photoshop Elements to try to find and retain the people in the photo for you, click the Highlight Skintones button in the options bar.

Figures 7.5-7.6
Move objects, people, or ducks closer together using the Recompose tool.

4. When you've painted the areas you care about, drag the handles in as far as you want. If you're happy with the results, click the green Commit button. If not, try painting additional areas to fine-tune the process.

 The handles are at the edge of the image itself, so if you've zoomed in, you may need to scroll to see them.

Using the Cookie Cutter tool

Crops don't have to be rectangular, thanks to the Cookie Cutter tool. You can use any of the shapes that come with Photoshop Elements to crop your photo.

1. Select the Cookie Cutter tool.

2. Display the Shapes menu in the options bar.

tip **To see all the shapes available, click the double arrow at the top of the window, and then choose All Elements Shapes.**

3. Select a shape and then close the menu.

tip **If you double-click a shape, the menu closes automatically.**

4. Select Crop in the options bar.

note If you want to keep the shape proportional or generate a shape with specific dimensions, select an option from the Shape Options menu in the options bar before drawing the shape.

5. Drag the cursor across your image to draw the shape. You can change the proportions of the shape or resize it by dragging the handles.

Figure 7.7 *Crops don't have to be rectangular!*

6. When you're happy with the cropped area, click the green Commit button.

note Some shapes display only small portions of your image. For example, the shapes in the Frames library show only what appears where the frame itself is located. For most purposes, you'll get the best results if you use a solid shape for cropping with the Cookie Cutter tool.

tip The Cookie Cutter tool works well if you want to create a digital matte for your image. After cropping, add a background layer of a solid color, a pattern, or a gradient to set it off.

Dividing a scanned image into multiple images

Scanning old photos can be tedious. It's faster if you place more than one photo on the scanning bed at once, but they're almost certain to slip a bit when you lower the lid. Photoshop Elements can divide the scanned image into individual photos, and it even does its best to straighten them, as well. (And its best is pretty darned good.)

 Make sure there's clear space between the photos on the scanning bed so Photoshop Elements can identify their borders.

To divide a scanned image into multiple images, open the scanned image in Photoshop Elements. Then choose Image > Divide Scanned Photos. That's all there is to it. Each image appears in its own image window.

 If your photos have white areas near the border, try placing a dark piece of paper over the photos when you scan them.

Transforming images

You can rotate, flip, skew, distort, and add perspective to an image, a selection, a layer, or a shape.

One thing to note, though: If you're trying to transform a Background layer, Photoshop Elements automatically converts it to a regular layer before transforming it.

Rotating or flipping an object or layer

If you can select it, you can rotate or flip it. Start by selecting the image, layer, selection, or shape that you want to rotate or flip. Then choose Image > Rotate, and choose the appropriate command to rotate to the left, right, half-turn, or a custom amount, or to flip horizontally or vertically. Note that there are commands specifically for rotating and flipping selections.

Figures 7.8-7.9-7.10
Rotate or flip an image instantly.

If you choose to rotate a custom amount, type the number of degrees of rotation. Positive numbers rotate clockwise; negative numbers rotate counterclockwise.

Rotating an item manually

If you're not sure how many degrees you want to rotate a layer or selection, rotate it manually.

1. Choose either Image > Rotate > Free Rotate Layer or Image > Rotate > Free Rotate Selection. Photoshop Elements displays a bounding box.

 The Free Rotate command isn't available if you've selected a Background layer. You need to rename it before you can transform it.

2. Click and drag the rotation handle at the bottom of the bounding box (the cursor should change to arrows) to rotate the object.

By default, the layer or selection rotates around the central axis. If you want it to rotate around a different axis, select it in the reference point locator in the options bar.

3. To apply the transformation, double-click inside the bounding box or click the green Commit button. Or you can just press Enter or Return.

Scaling an item

To scale a photo, layer, selection, or shape, first select it and then choose Image > Resize > Scale. Then, drag a corner handle to scale both height and width; to scale only one or the other, drag a side handle. If you want to keep the image proportional, select Constrain Proportions in the options bar. To apply the transformation, double-click inside the bounding box, click the Commit button, or press Enter or Return.

 You can also enter a percentage in the Width, the Height, or both in the options bar.

Skewing or distorting an item

You can slant a layer, selection, or image by skewing it. To stretch or squish something, distort it.

1. Select the image, layer, selection, or shape you want to skew or distort.

2. Choose Image > Transform > Skew, or Image > Transform > Distort. (If you've selected a shape, the command changes to Image > Transform Shape > Skew, or Image > Transform Shape > Distort.)

3. Drag a handle to modify the bounding box.

4. When you're happy with what you've got, double-click inside the bounding box, click the green Commit button, or press Enter.

Figure 7.11 *Skewing an image.*

Applying perspective

You can make an item appear to exist in three dimensions by adding perspective.

1. Select the item you want to add perspective to.

2. Choose Image > Transform > Perspective. (If you've selected a shape, it's Image > Transform Shape > Perspective.)

> **note** **The Background layer will become a regular layer.**

3. Drag a corner handle on the bounding box.

4. To accept the changes, double-click inside the bounding box, click the green Commit button, or press Enter or Return.

Figure 7.12 *Apply perspective to move the image through three dimensions.*

Making multiple transformations at once

The Free Transform command gives you access to all the transformation options at once. You can rotate, scale, skew, distort, and shift perspective in one fell swoop.

1. Select the item to transform.

2. Choose Image > Transform > Free Transform (or Image > Transform Shape > Free Transform Shape).

3. Transform!

   * To scale, drag any handle. (Press Shift as you drag if you want to keep it proportional.)

   * To rotate, move the pointer outside the bounding box until you see the curved arrows, and then drag. (Press Shift as you drag to constrain the rotation to 15 degree increments.)

   * To distort, press Ctrl (Windows) or Command (Mac OS) and drag any handle.

   * To skew, press Ctrl+Shift (Windows) or Command+Shift (Mac OS) and drag a handle in the middle of any side of the bounding box.

   * To apply perspective, press Ctrl+Alt+Shift (Windows) or Command+Option+Shift (Mac OS) and drag a corner handle.

4. When you're done, double-click inside the bounding box, click the green Commit button, or press Enter or Return.

Retouching

Sometimes, reality's not all it's cracked up to be—and sometimes a photo doesn't quite leave the subject looking like it did in real life. Photoshop Elements gives you plenty of tools to help you change your photos to reflect your view of how things ought to be.

Removing red eye

You can fix red eye in Full Edit or Quick Fix mode, and the Remove Red Eye tool works the same in both places. See Chapter 6 to learn how to use the tool.

Making small repairs

Maybe it's that pimple on your nose. Or it could be a smudge on your camera lens that showed up on the photo. When there's a small imperfection in your image, give the Spot Healing Brush a try. It's designed to take care of trouble spots quickly, "healing" them into the surrounding area.

1. Select the Spot Healing Brush tool.

2. Choose a brush size in the options bar. To heal the blemish with a single click, select a brush size that is slightly larger than the area you want to fix.

3. Select a Type option in the options bar: Proximity Match or Create Texture. The Proximity Match option uses just the edge pixels to find an image area to use as a patch; it's usually your best bet. The Create Texture option uses all the pixels in the area to create a texture for fixing the area.

 Remember that you can always undo and try the other option if the first one doesn't work as well as you'd like!

4. Click the area you want to fix. If it's a slightly larger area, click and drag the tool over it.

Fixing larger areas

Larger areas of concern require the Healing Brush. For this tool, you need to create a sample from an area that looks right. Then, drag the Healing Brush tool over the imperfections, and it blends the sample area with the surrounding content.

1. Select the Healing Brush tool.

2. Choose a brush size in the options bar.

3. Select a Mode. The Mode determines how the source blends with the pixels that were already there: Normal mode lays new pixels over the original; Replace mode preserves the film grain and texture at the edges of the brush stroke.

4. Select the source. You can use a pattern from the Pattern panel, but you're usually better off sampling pixels from an image.

5. Choose how pixels are sampled and applied. If Aligned is selected, the tool samples with the current sampling point (not the original point) even as you release the mouse button. If Aligned is not selected, the tool goes back to the original point to sample pixels each time you stop and resume painting.

6. Select whether to sample data from all layers, only the current layer, or just the current layer and below.

7. Position the tool where you want to start sampling, then Alt-click or Option-click to sample the data.

tip   **You can sample from any open image, not just the one you're painting in.**

8. Drag the tool over the flaw to meld existing data with sampled data. You can't tell exactly what it will look like until you release the mouse button; that's when the pixels meld.

Figures 7.13-7.14
The Healing Brush tool can help with large smudges in some photos.

tip If there is a strong contrast at the edges of the area you want to heal, the Healing Brush may heal from pixels that are a different color and texture. To prevent this, make a selection just slightly larger than the area you want to heal before you use the Healing Brush tool.

Cloning images or areas in an image

Cloning may be hotly debated in scientific and medical communities, but it's a real time-saver when you're retouching photos. Here's how it works: You take a sample from an area that's "clean" and then you paint that sample over a compromised area in the same image or in a different one. It's all done using the Clone Stamp tool.

1. Select the Clone Stamp tool.

2. Position the tool over the part of any open image that you want to sample, and then Alt-click or Option-click. That sets the sample.

3. Click the tool somewhere to stamp the full sample—or drag over an area to paint the sample in.

4. Drag the Clone Stamp tool over the area you want to repair.

Figures 7.15-7.16
Use the Clone Stamp tool to paint over an area with an area that's similar.

There are several settings in the options bar, but a couple of them deserve attention. The Aligned option changes how the sample is painted. If Aligned is selected, the Clone Stamp tool starts with the sample area when you begin painting, and as you continue painting, it moves out from the sample area. You could end up painting in artifacts you weren't expecting. If Aligned is not selected, the Clone Stamp tool starts again with the sample area every time you begin painting again, so there's uniformity as you paint.

Another option worth noting is the Sample All Layers option. By default, the Clone Stamp tool samples only the pixels in the active layer. If you select Sample All Layers, it copies the pixels from all the visible layers.

You can change the brush tip or size. You can also select a blending mode, which changes how the sample you're painting in blends with the pixels that were already there. (Normal mode just plops the pixels on top of the original pixels.) Change the opacity if you want to be able to see the original pixels through the cloned area.

Replacing colors

The Color Replacement tool does just what it claims to do. You can paint over a target color with any color you like, whether you're changing a hair color, the color of clothing, or the hue of the grass.

1. Select the Color Replacement tool. It's nested with the Brush tool.

2. Set up the brush and blending mode in the options bar.

 Generally, you'll get the best results if you use Color for the blending mode.

3. In the options bar, select Discontiguous to replace the sampled color any time the pointer moves over it; select Contiguous to replace only colors that are contiguous with the color immediately under the pointer.

4. Select an initial Tolerance setting. This determines how similar a color needs to be to the target color for it to be replaced. (A low percentage requires the colors to be very similar; a higher percentage replaces a broader range of colors.)

5. Select a foreground color to replace the color you don't want.

6. Click the color you want to replace.

7. Drag the tool over the area of the image to replace the targeted color. You may need to adjust the size of the brush and the tolerance as you work.

Replacing the background

Move the subject of your photo from a boring location to an exciting one—or perhaps simply one with a better background color. With a little finesse, you can pull just about any person or object out of a photo and ease them into any background you like.

There are several methods for replacing the background, but the basic procedure is the same for all of them. First, remove the existing background. Then, insert a new one.

The Magic Extractor and Background Eraser were both designed specifically for this task. Before they existed, photo editors relied on the Magic Wand tool and inverting selections to do the trick. We'll look at all of these methods.

The Magic Extractor

To use this feature, choose Image > Magic Extractor. In the Magic Extractor dialog box, your goal is to help Photoshop Elements distinguish the foreground (the part you want to keep) from the background (the part you want to remove). To do that, click on areas of the foreground using the Foreground Brush (the top one in the toolbox), and then click on areas of the background using the Background Brush (the second tool in the toolbox). The foreground dots are red; background dots are blue.

Figure 7.17 *Paint dots to guide the Magic Extractor feature.*

tip You can change the color of foreground and background dots—especially useful if your object or background is red or blue. Just double-click on the foreground or background color on the right side of the dialog box, and then select a new color.

When you've given the Magic Extractor some guidance, click Preview to see how it does. It's not a perfect tool—maybe not even magical—but it does a pretty good job, usually. If your image is complex, the task can be trickier.

 It can be easier to see how clean the selection is against a different color. Select Black Matte from the Background menu on the right to see the selection more clearly.

Figure 7.18 *For clearer viewing, preview the selection against a black matte.*

To clean up any stray bits, you can add more dots (foreground or background). You can also use the Selection Eraser to remove any parts of the background that are farther from your subject, or use the Add To Selection brush to paint in more of your foreground. The Point Eraser removes dots, in case you accidentally put some in the wrong area. There's also a Smoothing Brush to smooth the edges.

Use all of these tools to tidy up the selection, and then, when only the foreground is visible, click OK to close the Magic Extractor dialog box. What remains is the foreground.

The Background Eraser tool

The Background Eraser tool is a direct, but potentially awkward, way to turn a background transparent.

To use it, select the layer containing the areas you want to erase.

Then, select the Background Eraser tool. It's grouped with the Eraser tool. You can set the brush size in the options bar, and also choose whether it erases contiguous or discontiguous pixels—and what the tolerance is for color difference.

 If you selected the Background layer, Photoshop Elements automatically converts it to a regular layer when you use this tool.

As you drag the pointer, the crosshair in the icon indicates the hotspot. The pixels directly under the hotspot define the color the Background Eraser will remove within the circle. A higher tolerance value means the tool erases colors that are less similar; low tolerance means only colors that are very similar will be erased.

When you start working with the tool, use a large brush size and a high tolerance. Paint quickly over the areas of the background that aren't close to the foreground area you want to keep.

Figure 7.19 *Use a large brush size as you begin to erase the background.*

As you grow closer to the foreground area you want to keep, lower the tolerance. Then, carefully erase the rest of the background, making sure that the hotspot never covers areas you want to keep. The broader brush can overlap your foreground object, but if the pixels in the foreground object aren't similar to those in the hotspot, the foreground object won't be erased.

Other selection tools

You can use any selection tool you want, really. For some images, the Magic Wand tool may be the best bet (if either the background or foreground colors are very consistent). For others, the Quick Selection tool is a good option.

Remember, too, that you can select either the foreground object or the background—whichever is easier. If you select the foreground object, just choose Select > Inverse to switch to a background selection. Once the background is selected, delete it. Or you can copy the foreground selection onto a new layer—whichever you prefer.

Adding a new background

With the old background gone, you need only slip a new background behind your foreground in the layer stack. You can copy a layer from another image, or create a new fill layer in a solid color. You can also add an artistic background from the Content panel. Photoshop Elements comes with backgrounds that range from baseball diamonds to leopard prints. To apply one, just select the Background layer in the Layers panel and then drag the swatch from the Content panel onto your image.

Figure 7.20 *Pop in a background from another photo or a pattern from the content panel.*

Merging photos

When you want to combine the best parts of similar photos, the Photomerge features can make your life much easier. Photoshop Elements 8 includes several Photomerge features:

Photomerge Group Shot merges parts of multiple images, especially designed to capture everyone looking their best in group photos.

Photomerge Faces combines facial features from multiple people.

Photomerge Scene Cleaner eliminates unwanted objects.

Photomerge Exposure combines the best quality from images with different exposures.

Photomerge Panorama stitches together several images for a much broader view of a subject.

To use a Photomerge option in Full Edit mode, open the images you want to use so that they're all in the Project Bin. Then, choose File > New > Photomerge [feature], and follow the instructions. The screen you'll see provides exactly the same information as the one that appears in the Photomerge guided edit of the same name.

The only feature that's available in Full Edit mode but not Guided Edit mode is Photomerge Panorama. For help using the others, see Chapter 6.

Creating a panorama

To stitch together a panorama, start by opening the images you want to use in Photoshop Elements. That way you won't have to go hunting for them later.

1. Open the images you want to use in Photoshop Elements.

2. Choose File > New > Photomerge Panorama.

3. In the Photomerge dialog box, select Files from the Use menu and then click Add Open Files. Photoshop Elements lists the files you have open. If you have any files open that you don't want to include in the panorama, select them and click Remove.

4. Select a layout option in the Photomerge dialog box. Often, Auto does a great job. But you can select a different layout option. In fact, because the Photomerge feature creates a new file every time you run it, leaving your originals untouched, you can try different layout options to see which gives the best results for the set of images you're working with.

Figure 7.21 *Auto does a great job for most images; here, it's also the Perspective option.*

Figure 7.22 *These are the same images, using the Cylindrical option, which is often best for wide panoramas.*

Figure 7.23 *And the same image, with Reposition Only selected.*

note The Interactive Layout option can be a little daunting, especially if you want to change the vanishing point. Refer to Photoshop Elements Help for advice on using this option.

5. When you've selected a layout option, click OK. Photoshop Elements does its thing, and presto! You've got a panorama. You can crop it if necessary, or extend a background color to the edge using other techniques covered in this book. But the hardest part has been done for you!

Painting

In Full Edit mode, you can use painting tools to change the color of pixels in an image or modify existing colors. As with other tools, you can adjust settings for painting tools in the options bar—including (depending on the tool) brush size, blending modes, opacity, and airbrush effects.

The tools

There are several tools you can use to paint, erase, stamp, fill, or otherwise change the color of pixels in your image.

- The Brush tool acts like a traditional paintbrush. It paints the foreground color onto the image.

- The Pencil tool does the same thing as the Brush tool, except with hard-lined edges, like a pencil.

- The Impressionist Brush tool applies stylized brush strokes to existing color. You can change the style, area size, and tolerance options to simulate textures associated with different artistic styles.

- The Eraser tool removes color pixels from a layer. It either makes the pixels transparent, or, if you're working in a layer with transparency locked (such as the Background layer), it changes the pixels to the background color.

- The Magic Eraser tool changes all similar pixels to transparency; if you're working in a layer with transparency locked, it changes them to the background color. You can choose to erase contiguous pixels only, or all similar pixels on the current layer.

- The Background Eraser tool makes pixels transparent so that you can remove an object from its background. See page 136 for more on this tool.

- The Paint Bucket tool fills areas of the image with the foreground color or a pattern.

- The Pattern Stamp tool paints with a predefined pattern or a pattern you design.

- The Smudge tool picks up the color where the stroke begins and pushes it, as if you were dragging a finger through wet paint.

Setting brush options

You can select a brush preset from the Brushes menu in the options bar. Don't limit yourself to the default brushes either. There are several brush sets, including calligraphic brushes and even special effects brushes that make it easy to give someone a rose tattoo.

Fine-tune the brush you select by changing its brush size, changing the blending mode, or adjusting the opacity. Those settings alone can give you great flexibility. But they're only the beginning. You can set brush dynamics using a menu in the options bar. Click the paintbrush icon to see all your options.

- Fade sets the number of steps until the paint fades out. The lower the value, the faster the paint stroke fades away. If the value is 0, the stroke won't fade at all.

- Hue Jitter switches the stroke color between the foreground and background colors. The higher the value, the more frequently the color switches.

- Scatter distributes brush strokes irregularly. The higher the value, the greater the scatter.

- Spacing controls the distance between the brush marks in a stroke. For a dense, continuous stroke, keep the Spacing value low. (The value is a percentage of the brush diameter.) For a series of dots with space in between them, use a higher value.

Figure 7.24 *Combine a special effects brush, such as the butterfly, with spacing and scatter for cool effects.*

tip Spacing comes in handy if you're creating a consistent border across an image. Make sure Scatter is set to 0 and then set a high Spacing value with a special effects brush or a brush you create from an image.

- Hardness determines how firm the brush head is.

- Angle sets the angle by which the long axis of an elliptical brush is set off from the horizontal axis.

- Roundness is the ratio between the short and long axes. It's 100 percent for a circular brush; 0 percent for a linear brush.

Creating a custom brush shape

You can create custom brush shapes from selections or entire photos. Brushes you create are added to the bottom of the Brushes pop-up panel. Note, however, that the color in your selection is not included in the brush.

To create a custom brush shape from an area of a photo:

1. Select the part of the image you want to use.

2. Choose Edit > Define Brush From Selection.

3. Name the brush and click OK.

 You can also create a custom brush from a full image. To do that, deselect everything and then choose Edit < Define Brush.

Figures 7.25-7.26
Create your own brush shapes in Photoshop Elements.

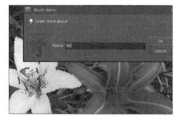

Filling a layer with a color or pattern

To fill an entire layer quickly, select a foreground color, select the layer, and then choose Edit > Fill Layer. You can select a color from the Use menu, or choose Pattern and then select a pattern.

Alternatively, you can select the foreground color in the toolbox, and then select the Paintbucket tool and click on the new layer to fill the entire thing.

> **tip** You can create a custom pattern. To do so, make a rectangular selection of an area, and make sure Feather is set to o pixels. (Or, to create a pattern from the entire image, deselect everything.) Then, choose Edit > Define Pattern or Edit > Define Pattern From Selection. Name the pattern, and click OK. Your custom pattern will appear in the Pattern Picker the next time you open it.

Fill layers create an entire layer with a solid color, a gradient, or a pattern fill. Fill layers don't affect the layers below them, but you can't paint on a fill layer unless you simplify it.

To create a fill layer, select the layer above which you want to place the fill layer. Then, click the New Fill Or Adjustment Layer button at the bottom of the Layers panel and choose a fill type (Solid Color, Gradient, or Pattern). Set the options, and click OK.

Outlining objects on a layer

To quickly add a colored outline around a selection or the content of a layer, select the area or layer. Then, choose Edit > Stroke (Outline) Selection. Set options in the Stroke dialog box to determine the width, color, blending mode, and so on for the stroke, and then click OK.

Working with gradients

A gradient is a stretch of pixels that begins with one color and ends with another, gradually moving from one to the other. Or, it could move through several colors, depending on the settings you choose.

You can create different kinds of gradients: Linear gradients move in a straight line; Radial gradients shade from the center of a circle to the outside (or vice versa); Angle gradients shade counterclockwise around the starting point; Reflected gradients use symmetric linear gradients on either side of a starting point; and Diamond gradients shade outward from the starting point in a diamond pattern.

Figures 7.27–7.28–7.29–7.30–7.31
*Types of gradients:
Linear, Radial,
Angle, Reflected,
and Diamond*

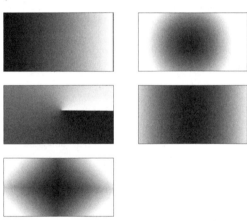

To apply a gradient:

1. Select the area you want to fill. (If you don't make a selection, the gradient is applied to the entire active layer.)

2. Select the Gradient tool.

3. Select the type of gradient you want to use in the options bar.

4. Choose a gradient fill from the Gradient Picker panel in the options bar to use as the base for your gradient.

5. If the gradient you've selected is the one you want to use, skip to Step 7. Otherwise, click Edit to define your own gradient.

6. In the Gradient Editor dialog box, you'll see the color stops for the selected gradient underneath the gradient bar. Customize them:

   * To change the color of a color stop, double-click it and select a different color in the Color Picker.

   * To move a color stop, drag it to the left or right.

   * To add a color stop, click below the gradient bar.

   * To change the transition midpoint between colors, drag the diamond below the gradient bar to the right or the left.

   * To delete a color stop, select it and press Delete.

Figure 7.32 *The Gradient Editor.*

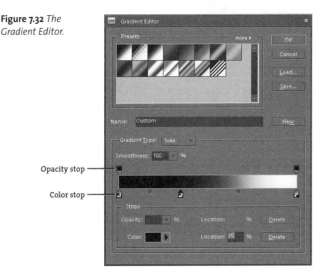

7. Next, customize the opacity stops, which appear above the gradient bar and determine the opacity at each point of the gradient. To change it, select an opacity stop and change the Opacity value.

tip Once you have your gradient settings, you can save them to use another time. Click Save and name them; they'll appear in the Gradient Picker panel the next time you open it.

8. Click OK to accept the gradient settings.

9. Set gradient options in the options bar, including the blending mode and opacity. Reverse switches the order of the colors.

10. Drag across the image or selection to set the starting point and the ending point of the gradient.

Adding shapes

You can add shapes such as rectangles or ellipses to your image using any of the shape tools in Photoshop Elements. There are a couple of important things to know about shapes you create.

First, when you create a shape, Photoshop Elements creates a new layer for it. So the shape itself and any modifications you make to it don't affect the original image. A shape layer can have more than one shape on it.

Second, shapes are vector graphics. They're made of lines and curves instead of pixels. Because vector graphics are resolution-independent, you can move, resize, or do just about anything else to them without losing quality.

To change the color of a shape, edit its fill layer or apply a layer style. Shapes are great if you're preparing something as a web page; they make good buttons, navigation bars, and so on.

Shape tools

Some of the shape tools are self-explanatory. For example, the Rectangle tool draws rectangles. The Ellipse tool draws ellipses. For a perfect square, press the Shift key as you draw with the Rectangle tool; for a perfect circle, press Shift as you draw with the Ellipse tool.

Other shape tools are a little more complex. The Rounded Rectangle tool draws rectangles with rounded corners; the Radius setting in the options bar determines how rounded the corners will be. (The higher the Radius value, the more rounded the corners.)

Figure 7.33 *For rounded corners, change the Radius value.*

The Polygon tool draws multi-sided shapes of many sorts. It's the tool to use to draw a triangle or an octagon. You can also draw stars using this tool: Click the arrow next to the polygon icon to see a menu. Then, select Star. Now when you draw a shape, the sides are indented toward the middle, like a star. If you select Smooth Corners, you get more of a flower effect. Play around with all the options to see what's available to you.

Figure 7.34 *With the Polygon tool, you can create shapes of many different sides and angles.*

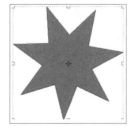

The Line tool draws lines. Change the weight of the line in the options bar. You can put an arrowhead on a line: Click next to the line icon to see the Arrowheads menu. Select Start to put the arrowhead on the end of the line you start drawing; select End to put it on the other end of the line. Select both to have arrowheads on both ends. The Width and Length of the arrowheads are specified as a percentage of the line weight; you can also change the concavity of the arrowheads.

The Custom Shape tool

The Custom Shape tool works just like the Cookie Cutter tool, except instead of cropping the image, it paints a shape on a new layer.

To use the Shape tool:

1. Select the Custom Shape tool in the toolbox.

2. Select a shape from the Shapes menu in the options bar.

Figure 3.35 *Photoshop Elements comes with many shapes.*

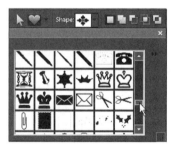

3. Select a color for the shape.

4. Select a style for the shape.

5. Draw the shape. Photoshop Elements creates a new layer for it.

You can continue to modify the shape by changing the layer style applied in the options bar. You can also move the layer up or down in the Layers panel. For example, if you're using a frame shape to frame an image, you probably want the shape layer to be at the top of the layer stack. If you're using a shape as a background to an image, you probably want it to be at the bottom of the stack.

 Don't forget about blending modes, which change how the shape layer interacts with the layers beneath it. Experiment to see what you can do.

Creating multiple shapes on one layer

Photoshop Elements creates a new layer each time you draw a new shape. But you can add multiple shapes to a single layer. To do so, draw your first shape and then select a shape option in the options bar to determine how the shapes will interact (add, subtract, intersect, or exclude). Then, draw your shape. The shapes don't have to be near each other, but if they are, the shape option determines how they affect each other.

Figure 7.36 *The shape option determines how shapes interact with each other.*

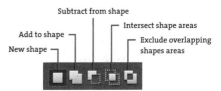

Subtract from shape
Intersect shape areas
Add to shape
Exclude overlapping shapes areas
New shape

- Add combines the two shapes into one shape area. (The shapes remain distinct if you select them with the Shape Selection tool.)

- Subtract hides the area where the shapes overlap.

- Intersect hides all but the area where the shapes intersect.

- Exclude removes the overlapping areas in new and existing shapes.

Adding text

You can add captions to photos, design titles, or include commentary on your photos in Full Edit mode. Use the Horizontal Type and Vertical Type tools to create and edit text. Photoshop Elements creates a new layer for text, so you can work with it separately from other objects.

Typing text in Photoshop Elements isn't quite like typing in a word processor or other application. You can create a single line of text or paragraph text. To create a single line, just click where you want the text to appear and start typing. (When you're creating single lines of text, press Enter or Return to start a new line.) To create paragraph text, which will wrap from one line to the next, drag a rectangle with the tool to create a text box, and then type into it.

Figure 7.37 *Type text onto a new layer in your image.*

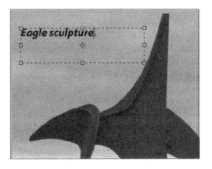

While you're in text edit mode, you can format the text using options in the options bar. Select a font, style, type size, alignment, and color. When you're done editing the text, click the green Commit button, click outside the text, or select a different tool.

Try selecting Anti-aliased in the options bar to make text appear smoother.

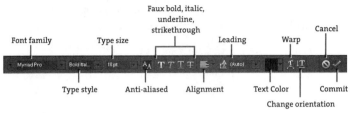

Figure 7.38 *Text options.*

Editing type

Type you've created has its own layer. You can apply layer styles and other layer commands to the layer, just as you would to any other. To edit the text itself, select the layer and then select one of the type tools.

> **tip** You can also double-click the text box with the Move tool to select the layer and switch tools.

> **note** Horizontal text flows left to right; vertical text flows top to bottom.

To make changes, click the insertion point and add text or select the text you want to edit and then type replacement text. You can also select text and change the formatting.

> **note** Working with Asian type is a little different from working with Roman characters. Photoshop Elements does support Asian type. See Photoshop Elements Help for the ins and outs.

Warp type

For some additional fun, you can distort type to conform to different shapes, such as an arc or a wave. There are a couple of limitations: Everything on the text layer is affected, so you can't warp individual characters. And if you've applied the faux Bold to the text, you can't warp it.

1. Select a type tool, and click the Warp button in the options bar.

2. Choose a warp style from the Style pop-up menu. This is where you decide whether you want to squeeze or plump the text. You can see the text change as soon as you select a style.

3. Select an orientation: Horizontal or Vertical. Then fine-tune it, if you like, specifying how much it should bend, and horizontal and vertical distortions.

4. Click OK when you have the effect you want.

Figures 7.39-7.40 *You can easily warp text.*

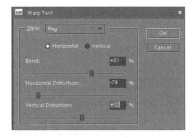

If you change your mind later, you can remove the warping from the text. Just select the layer and a type tool. Then click the Warp button in the options bar again, choose None from the Style pop-up menu, and click OK.

Bonus: Using type as a mask

You can use text as a shape, whether you want to peek at images through text cutouts or paste the selected text into a new image.

1. Select the layer where you want the selection to appear. Don't select a text layer.

2. Select either the Horizontal Type Mask tool or the Vertical Type Mask tool.

3. Select formatting options in the options bar.

4. Type your text.

Figure 7.41 *The type mask tools select the letter shapes.*

The type selection border appears on the image layer. Now you can use it the same way you use any other selection. You can invert the selection, delete it, move it to another layer, whatever you want to do.

Figure 7.42 *Mask, invert, delete, ta-da!*

8

Applying Adjustments and Filters

Sometimes, you just need to pop in to Photoshop Elements to remove red eye, or maybe you only want to replace a background. But if you're looking to be truly creative, get to know the range of filters, effects, and adjustments you can apply in Photoshop Elements.

You've already learned a little bit about adjustment layers if you've used Quick Fix mode or made the retouching changes described in Chapter 7. In this chapter, I'll show you more about adjustment layers and all the options available to you there. Then, hold on to your hat as we dive into the vast array of filters you can apply to any image.

About adjustment layers

Adjustment layers let you safely play with color and tonal changes. You can change your image significantly, but because you're working with an adjustment layer, you can easily hide or edit those changes. By default, an adjustment layer affects all the layers below it.

You can apply the same opacity and blending mode settings to adjustment and fill layers as to image layers. And you can rearrange them in the Layers panel. Photoshop Elements names adjustment layers for the type of adjustment (such as Saturation), and fill layers for the type of fill (such as Gradient), but you can rename them if you want to.

Types of adjustment layers

Primarily, adjustment layers in Photoshop Elements modify the color and tonal values in an image. You can create the following kinds of adjustment layers:

- Levels corrects tonal values.

- Brightness/Contrast lightens or darkens.

- Hue/Saturation adjusts colors and their intensity.

- Gradient Map maps the grayscale range of an image to the colors in the selected gradient.

- Photo Filter adjusts color balance and temperature.

- Invert creates a negative based on brightness values.

- Threshold renders the image in pure black and pure white, with no gray, so you can find the lightest and darkest areas.

- Posterize reduces the number of levels in the image, thereby reducing the number of colors and flattening the appearance.

Creating an adjustment layer

Photoshop Elements automatically creates an adjustment layer when you use the Smart Brush or Detail Smart Brush tool, or when you apply many of the quick fixes.

To create an adjustment layer manually, select the top layer you want to affect in the Layers panel. Then, click the Create Adjustment Layer button at the bottom of the Layers panel and choose one of the adjustment types. Set options for the adjustment in the Adjustments panel.

Figure 8.1 *Click the Create Adjustment Layer button and select a type of adjustment.*

To affect just a portion of the image, make a selection before creating the adjustment layer.

Editing an adjustment layer

To edit an existing adjustment layer, double-click its thumbnail in the Layers panel. (Note: Don't click the white box. Click the leftmost thumbnail.) Make the changes, and click OK.

Figure 8.2 *The left thumbnail selects the adjustment layer; the right thumbnail selects the layer mask.*

A layer mask hides portions of a layer. You can use a mask to show or hide sections of an image or effect. Adjustment layers include layer masks automatically; that's what that white box is next to the layer thumbnail. To restrict the adjustment to a portion of the image, paint black over the areas you don't want affected by the adjustment. (White areas are affected; black areas are not.)

To paint the mask, select the adjustment layer and then use any painting or editing tool to paint over part of the image.

If you paint areas you didn't mean to, paint over them in white.

To see only the mask, Alt-click or Option-click the Layer Mask's thumbnail.

To see other layers again, Alt-click or Option-click the thumbnail again.

Using clipping masks

Remember when I said an adjustment layer usually affects all the layers beneath it? You can restrict which layers are affected by using a clipping mask. The bottom layer in the group determines the visible boundaries of the entire group. Layers have to be in order to be grouped. You can identify a clipping group because the bottom layer in the group is underlined and the thumbnails for the layers above it are indented and have a clipping group icon.

To create a clipping group, select the top layer of a pair of layers you want to group and choose Layer > Create Clipping Mask. The layers in the clipping group have the opacity and mode attributes of the bottom layer in the group.

Figure 8.3 *Because of the clipping group, the adjustment layer affects only the gradient layer directly beneath it.*

To remove a layer from a clipping group, select it and then choose Layer > Release Clipping Mask.

Adjusting lighting

Lighting problems are common for most amateur photographers. Frankly, we just don't have the skill, patience, or expensive equipment that professionals have. And how much time do you have to set up lighting when you want to catch a toddler with a spoon on her nose or a cat stalking a moth? The ideal is to have perfect lighting when you snap the photo, but we don't live in an ideal world. So we have Photoshop Elements and its adjustments instead. Levels, Shadows/Highlights, and Brightness/Contrast adjustments can usually shine a light on the details and remove the glare of a too-bright area.

tip You can apply these adjustments quickly using Quick Fix mode, Guided Edits mode, or the Smart Brush tool, as well. Quick fixes are covered in Chapter 5, guided edits in Chapter 6, and the Smart Brush tool on page 171 in this chapter.

Using Levels adjustments

The Levels controls are powerful, and they may be a little intimidating if you're not used to looking at histograms and talking about tonal levels. But once you understand what the Levels controls are doing, they can work wonders for you.

Start by making a selection on the part of your image that you want to adjust, or select the entire layer. Then click the Add Adjustment Layer button at the bottom of the Layers panel, and select Levels.

The Levels controls appear in the Adjustments panel. At the top of the panel, you see the channel that's displayed. Colors in an image each have their own channel, so an RGB image has a red channel, a green channel, and a blue channel, as well as an RGB channel. You can make adjustments to each.

Figure 8.4 *The Adjustments panel for Levels.*

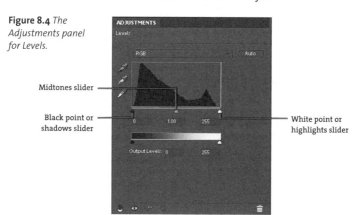

Midtones slider

Black point or shadows slider

White point or highlights slider

The Input Levels box shows a histogram, which represents the tonal values in your image. On the left are the shadows, and on the right are the highlights. In the middle are the midtones, the values that fall somewhere between shadow and highlight.

The black slider sets the black point for the image. That's the point at which everything darker is considered pure black. Move the black slider to the right, to the edge of the first group of pixels on the left side of the histogram. Dragging the black slider to the right darkens the photo a little.

The white slider sets the white point for the image. That's the point at which everything lighter is considered pure white. Drag the white slider to the left, to the edge of the first group of pixels on the right side of the histogram. Dragging the white slider to the left lightens the photo a little.

The black point and white point are important because Photoshop Elements uses them as a reference to determine the darkness of every other color in the image. You typically want to place the black point where the first group of pixels is located on the left, and move the white point to the first group of pixels on the right. If you move the black point closer to the middle, you lose, or *clip*, shadow detail. If you move the white point closer to the middle, you clip highlight detail.

Figure 8.5 *Drag the black and white points to the first group of pixels on each side.*

 To see which data you're clipping, if any, Alt-drag or Option-drag the black and white sliders. Colored areas show clipping.

To adjust the brightness of the midtones without changing the black and white values, drag the gray slider either direction.

When you're satisfied with the changes you've made, you can close the Adjustments panel or just move on to your next task. To see the difference you've made, hide the Levels layer in the Layers panel.

Using the Shadows/Highlights adjustment

You can also adjust shadows and highlights using a Shadows/Highlights adjustment. Unfortunately, there is no Shadows/Highlights adjustment layer, so to edit nondestructively, you're better off using the Levels adjustment layer. But sometimes you can get slightly different results using a Shadows/Highlights adjustment. Just make sure you're working on a copy of your image, not the original!

1. Make a selection or select the layer you want to affect.

2. Choose Enhance > Adjust Lighting > Shadows/Highlights.

3. Move the sliders to lighten shadows, darken highlights, or change the contrast level in the midtones.

4. Click OK when you're satisfied with the results.

Figure 8.6 *The Shadows/Highlights adjustment lets you brighten shadows, darken highlights, and adjust the midtones using sliders.*

Using the Brightness/Contrast adjustment layer

While this option isn't as good at making tonal adjustments, it's great for adjusting the brightness or contrast in part of an image—or even an entire image.

Make a selection or select the topmost layer of those you want to affect. Click the New Adjustment Layer button at the bottom of the Layers panel, and choose Brightness/Contrast.

In the Adjustments panel, drag the sliders to adjust the brightness and contrast. Dragging to the left decreases the brightness or contrast; dragging to the right increases it.

Figure 8.7 *Tweak the brightness and contrast using an adjustment layer.*

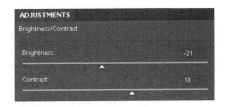

Figure 8.8 *Before.*

Figure 8.9 *After.*

tip You can also darken and lighten specific areas of an image with the Dodge and Burn tools. The Dodge tool brings out shadow detail, and the Burn tool brings out highlight detail. I'm not a real fan of these tools, because I find them a little awkward and imprecise (or perhaps because I'm awkward and imprecise), but you can try them and see how they work for you.

Adjusting color

Color is a big deal in photographs. If the color isn't quite right, a healthy person can look sickly, a sunny day can appear stormy, and an exciting event can look dull and uninteresting. So it's important. It's difficult to show color in the grayscale photos of this book, so I encourage you to experiment with your own photos to see how these techniques work.

Removing color casts

A color cast is an unwanted tint that distorts the mood and tone of an image. You can remove a color cast several different ways in Photoshop Elements. You might start with a quick fix (see Chapter 5) or the Remove Color Cast guided edit (see Chapter 6). But there are options in Full Edit mode as well. You can use the Color Variations dialog box to select the correct tone, let Photoshop Elements take a stab at it with the Remove Color Cast adjustment, or, if you're very savvy, create a Levels adjustment layer.

To automatically remove a color cast, choose Enhance > Adjust Color > Remove Color Cast. Then, click an area in your image that should be white, black, or neutral gray. You can click different areas until the adjustment seems right. Click OK to accept the changes.

The Color Variations dialog box isn't a precise way to remove a color cast, but if you're working with an obvious cast, it might do the trick. To compare variations and select the appropriate tone, choose Enhance > Adjust Color > Color Variations. You'll see the Before and After images. Select whether you want to try adjusting midtones, shadows, highlights, or saturation, and then move the Adjust Color slider to change the amount of adjustment. Then click one of the thumbnails to increase or decrease a particular color, lighten or darken the image, or, if you're adjusting saturation, to increase or decrease saturation. You can click Undo to move backwards. When you're satisfied with your adjustments, click OK.

Figure 8.10 *The Color Variations dialog box lets you increase or decrease specific colors and lighten or darken the image.*

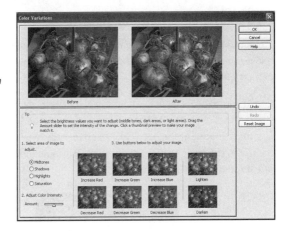

note The Color Variations command is not available if you're working with an image in Indexed Color mode.

For best results using the Levels adjustment layer to remove a color cast, you should have some idea of whether you want to add red, green, or blue to the image to balance it. To remove a color cast using a Levels adjustment layer, start by clicking the New Adjustment Layer button in the Layers panel and choosing Levels. Then, in the Adjustments panel, choose a color channel from the Channel pop-up menu. Choose Red if you want to add red or cyan to the image, Green to add green or magenta, and Blue to add blue or yellow. Drag the middle input slider to add or subtract color.

tip You can also use the gray eyedropper in the Levels dialog box to remove a color cast. Double-click the eyedropper and make sure the RGB values are equal in the Color Picker. After you close the Color Picker, click an area in your image that should be a neutral gray.

Changing color saturation or hue

The color saturation determines how vivid the color is, while the hue determines the actual color. You can modify both of these qualities using a Hue/Saturation adjustment layer.

Click the New Adjustment Layer button in the Layers panel, and then choose Hue/Saturation. In the Adjustments panel, move the Hue, Saturation, and Lightness sliders. At the bottom of the panel are two color bars. The top bar shows the original color, and the lower bar shows how the adjustment affects all hues at full saturation.

Figure 8.11 *The Adjustments panel for a Hue/ Saturation layer.*

By default, Master is selected in the Edit pop-up menu, so you're adjusting all colors at once. You can adjust only the Greens, Yellows, Cyans, or another color, if you want to. You can select which color to edit from the Edit menu, or you can move the sliders between the color bars at the bottom of the panel.

note If you want to affect only saturation, you can use the Sponge tool. Select it in the toolbox, and then drag it over part of the image to increase or decrease saturation, depending on the mode you've selected in the options bar.

Adjusting skin tone

Skin tones are a priority in images where people are the subjects. Note, though, that to adjust skin tone, you have to adjust the overall color in the photo. You can use the Adjust Skin Tone guided edit (see Chapter 6). Or, you can use a feature in Full Edit mode that does the same thing.

To adjust skin tone in Full Edit mode:

1. Choose Enhance > Adjust Color > Adjust Color for Skin Tone.

2. Click an area of skin. Make sure Preview is selected so you can see the changes Photoshop Elements made.

Figure 8.12 *Click the eyedropper on an area of skin.*

3. If you want to fine-tune changes, drag the Tan, Blush, or Temperature sliders. Tan changes the level of brown, Blush changes the level of red, and Temperature changes the overall color of skin tones.

4. When you're satisfied, click OK.

Converting a color image to black and white

If you need to convert a color photograph to black and white (or, really, grayscale), you can use a quick and dirty, but often quite effective, method. Or, you can make a more precise conversion.

To make the conversion quickly, choose Enhance > Adjust Color > Remove Color. The result is the same as if you'd set Saturation to -100 in the Hue/Saturation dialog box. The overall brightness remains the same.

 To desaturate only part of an image, you can make a selection before choosing Remove Color.

If you're fussier about your conversion, use the Convert To Black And White command instead.

1. Select an area or a layer to convert; if nothing is selected, the entire image is converted.

2. Choose Enhance > Convert to Black and White.

3. Select a style option appropriate for your image, such as Portraits or Scenic Landscape.

4. Drag the Adjustment Intensity sliders to adjust the red, green, blue, or contrast data from the original color channels.

5. If you're happy with the results, click OK.

Figure 8.13 *For more control over a conversion, use the Convert to Black and White command.*

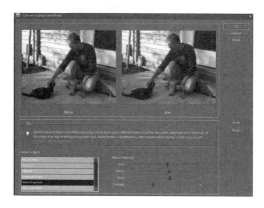

Applying adjustments with the Smart Brush tools

The Smart Brush tool applies color and tonal adjustments to specific areas of the image. It may seem like you're painting the adjustment on, but in fact, the Smart Brush is combining three steps in one: It's making a selection *and* creating an adjustment layer *and* specifying settings for that adjustment layer all at the same time.

The Smart Brush tool and the Detail Smart Brush tool are a little different in the way they make the selection. The Smart Brush tool works somewhat like the Quick Selection tool in that it guesses what you want to select. That's great if you're selecting a large or very consistent area. But if you're really trying to whiten teeth, it can be awfully challenging to keep all the gums and lips out of the selection. The Detail Smart Brush tool creates a mask only where you actually paint—there's no selection marquee hopping around. This is the tool to use for detail work.

To use the Smart Brush tool or the Detail Smart Brush tool, select the tool and then select an adjustment from the menu that pops up from the options bar. You can brighten an area overall, change the contrast, make parts of the image black and white, add a sepia tone, make blue skies brighter, whiten teeth, add "lipstick," and brighten the greenery. (Several of these options sound familiar, don't they? They're the same tasks you accomplish with tools that are available only in Quick Fix mode.)

tip **Though the adjustments are named for specific tasks, you can use them for other things. The Pearly Whites option doesn't recognize teeth. It's just adding a solid color fill layer, with a color that looks like brighter teeth, the Soft Light blending mode, and an opacity of 50 percent.**

Figure 8.14 *Select an adjustment from the menu in the options bar.*

These tools are handy, especially for intensifying sky color, quickly creating a black-and-white or sepia tone image, or making parts of an image brighter overall. And once you understand what the Smart Brush tools are doing, you can use them to create other effects, as well, with simple changes to the opacity or blending mode or fill color. As with all other adjustment or fill layers, double-click on the first thumbnail in the layer to make any changes to the adjustment or fill options.

Using filters

Filters can be practical or fun. You can use them to retouch photos, of course. But you can also use them to turn an everyday photo into a "painted" masterpiece.

tip You don't need to apply filters directly to your picture. You can apply them to solid-color or grayscale layers, generating a variety of backgrounds and textures, which you can then blur or otherwise distort. Then, use the texture as a background for your image, changing the blending mode and opacity for a subtle effect.

There are too many filters to go into detail about them all here, but the good folks at Adobe have described them all in Photoshop Elements Help, and I recommend taking a stroll through the list there. Filters come in several categories.

You can apply a filter using the Effects panel, the Filter menu, or the Filter Gallery. No matter which method you choose, start by making a selection or selecting the layer you want to apply the filter to.

Effects panel

If the Effects panel isn't open, choose Window > Effects. Then select a filter category, and double-click the filter you want to apply. Or, you can drag the filter onto the image or selection.

Figure 8.15 *The Effects panel.*

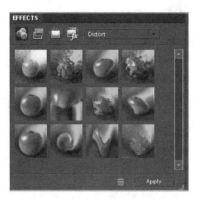

Filter menu

Choose Filter, then choose the filter category, and finally, the filter itself that you want to apply. If the filter name ends with an ellipsis (...), either a Filter Options dialog box or the Filter Gallery opens. Enter values or select options in the dialog box.

note If the Filter Options dialog box opens, it may also have a Preview option. Select Preview to see how settings change the effect before you commit to them. If there are sliders, you can also press Alt or Option while you drag a slider to see a real-time preview.

Filter Gallery

There are dozens of filters. If you're not sure which one you want to apply, the Filter Gallery can be a real time-saver. The Filter Gallery makes it easy to preview a filter's effect and either apply it or move on to the next one.

1. To open the Filter Gallery, make a selection or select an entire layer.

2. Choose Filter > Filter Gallery.

note Not all filters are shown in the Filter Gallery. The Blur filters, for example, aren't available in the gallery. Also, you cannot apply Photo Effects or layer styles from the Filter Gallery.

Figure 8.16
Try filters on for size in the Filter Gallery.

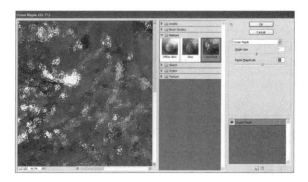

3. Click on filters until you find one you want to keep.

4. Adjust the settings to see what each filter can do for you. As you select filters, they appear in the list on the right; if you move on to the next one, it replaces the previous filter.

5. To apply a filter, click the New Effect Layer button at the bottom of the window.

    The filter you selected is applied, and you can continue to apply additional filters. You can return to filters you've already applied and adjust their settings, and you can rearrange the order of filters to change the way they interact with each other.

note Not all filters work on all images. For example, you can't use some filters on images in grayscale mode. No filters work on images in bitmap or indexed-color mode. And some filters don't work on 16-bit images.

6. When you've applied all the filters you want, click OK. If you want to exit the Filter Gallery without applying any filters, click Cancel.

tip Filters can be memory-intensive. You can free up memory on your computer by closing other applications. You can also try filters and settings on a smaller area, and apply them to the entire image only when you're certain what settings you want to use.

Sharpening and blurring images

Sharpening an image focuses soft edges and increases clarity; blurring an image softens hard edges and can minimize flaws. The key with either sharpening or blurring is to do just the right amount to enhance the image without either losing the detail or giving the photo a grainy look.

Sharpening an image

You can sharpen an image in four different ways: applying the Auto Sharpen command, using the Sharpen tool, adjusting the sharpness, or applying the Unsharp Mask Filter.

The Auto Sharpen command applies a minimal amount of sharpening, so that you can increase the clarity or focus of the image without over-sharpening it. To apply the Auto Sharpen command, make a selection and choose Enhance > Auto Sharpen. To apply it to the entire image, deselect everything before choosing the command.

The Sharpen tool focuses soft edges in the areas where you drag the tool. To avoid oversharpening, set a lower Strength value in the options bar. You can also set the size of the brush and the blending mode. If you want the sharpening to affect all visible layers, select Sample All Layers; deselect it to sharpen only the active layer. Then just drag the tool over the areas of the image you want to sharpen. If you want to sharpen an area more, drag the tool over it again.

The Adjust Sharpness command is an adjustment, but it doesn't create an adjustment layer. Therefore, changes you make using this adjustment do affect the underlying image. However, the Adjust Sharpness dialog box gives you more control than either the Auto Sharpen command or the Sharpen tool. Just be careful not to oversharpen.

To apply it:

1. Choose Enhance > Adjust Sharpness.

2. Click Select Preview so you can see how the changes you make affect the image.

3. Set the amount of sharpening, the radius, the sharpening algorithm, and the angle. The radius determines how many pixels surrounding

the edge pixels are affected—a higher radius makes sharpening more obvious. For the sharpening algorithm, Lens Blur detects edges and detail for finer sharpening, while Motion Blur attempts to reduce the effects of blur due to movement. (If you were going to use Gaussian Blur, use the Unsharp Mask filter instead of the Adjust Sharpness command). Select an angle only if you're removing motion blur.

Figure 8.17 *The Adjust Sharpness dialog box.*

4. Select More Refined if you want to process the file slowly for more accurate sharpening.

5. Click OK when you're happy with the preview.

The Unsharp Mask filter is a filter, but it's not in the Filter Gallery or the Effects panel. It sharpens edges in an image using a more traditional film technique. It locates the pixels that differ from surrounding pixels, and increases pixels' contrast. Within the specified radius, lighter pixels get lighter and darker pixels get darker.

tip You'll see the effects of the Unsharp Mask filter more prominently onscreen than you will in a high-resolution printed piece. If you're going to be printing to a high-quality printer, you may need to experiment to see what settings work best for print for your image.

To use the Unsharp Mask filter:

1. Select an image, layer, or area.

2. Choose Enhance > Unsharp Mask.

3. Select the Preview option so you can see how the changes you make affect your image.

Figure 8.18 *The Unsharp Mask dialog box.*

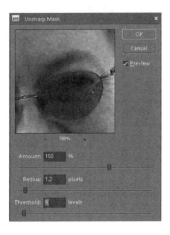

4. Set the amount of sharpening, the radius, and the threshold. For high-resolution printed images, try an amount between 150 percent and 200 percent. The radius determines the number of pixels to sharpen around edges (usually between 1 and 2). The threshold determines how far pixels must be from the surrounding area to be considered edge pixels. (Experiment with threshold values between 2 and 20.)

5. Click OK when you're satisfied.

Blurring an image

You can blur parts of an image using the Blur tool or one of many blur filters. The Blur tool is a quick way to reduce detail in a part of an image. However, blur filters give you much more control over how Photoshop Elements softens edge pixels.

The Blur tool is an excellent choice if you want to blur a background in order to bring the subject of your photo into greater focus. It can also be useful if you just want to blur some specific edges in your photo. To use it, select the Blur tool and then drag it across the areas of the image that you want to blur. You can specify the tool size, blending mode, and strength in the options bar, as well as whether you want the blurring to affect all layers or only the active layer.

To apply one of the blur filters, choose Filter > Blur > [filter].

The Blur and Blur More filters soften a selection of an image. They average the color values of pixels next to the hard edges of defined lines and shaded areas. Use the Blur filter to eliminate noise where there are significant color transitions. The Blur More filter produces an effect several times stronger than that of the Blur filter. Before you apply either the Blur or Blur More filter, make sure transparency isn't locked for the image layer.

The Gaussian Blur filter adds low-frequency detail and can produce a hazy effect. You can set the blur radius in the filter to determine how great the effect is.

The Motion Blur filter adds blur that approximates the blur that comes from the movement of the photo subject. You can set the angle and distance of the blur.

Figure 8.19 *You can add motion blur to part of an image to indicate motion.*

The Radial Blur filter adds blur that simulates the blur of a zooming or rotating camera. You can specify a spin, which blurs along concentric circular lines, or a zoom, which blurs along radial lines.

The Smart Blur filter is more precise than many others, and you have significant control over the blur. For example, you can set a mode for the edges of color transitions (Edge Only or Overlay Edge).

The Surface Blur filter preserves the edges while it blurs other areas of the image. It's a good filter for removing noise and graininess.

The Average filter fills the image or selection with the average color of the image or selection for a smooth look. Use this only if you want to blur a field of grass or a stretch of sky or some similarly consistent area.

9

Saving and Sharing Photos

You've removed color cast and fixed red eye, cropped and rotated, fixed the lighting and added effects. What now? You almost certainly want to save the improved image, probably with a new file name. And then? You can print it, share it on your website or Photoshop.com, combine it with other photos in an album for the web or on a CD, purchase professional prints, load it onto a digital picture frame, or create more complex projects such as calendars and photo books. Really, there's no reason to just keep your favorite photos on your hard drive, where you look at them every now and again. Good photos are meant to be seen!

Saving edited images

I hope you've been saving your work as you go, but once you've finished editing, you really have little choice. It's either save the image or lose all the work you've done. It's a good idea to keep a copy of your image in Photoshop (PSD) format, retaining all the layers, so that you can return to make changes later if you want to. If you're editing many images, I recommend storing the full PSD versions of your photos on a portable hard drive or other removable storage device. The file sizes can be quite large, and they add up quickly. To keep your computer tidy and nimble, off-site (but readily accessible) storage is a good idea.

In addition to your PSD copy, you'll probably want to save a version of the image with a much smaller file size, so that you can share it through email or on the web, print it faster, or load it onto a digital picture frame efficiently.

Selecting a file format

The most common and flexible formats for digital images are JPEG, TIFF, and PNG. In addition to these formats, you can save files in BMP, GIF, PCX, PDF, Photoshop EPS, Pict, Pixar, Photoshop Raw, Scitex CT, TGA (Targa), and other formats. Photoshop Elements Help does a good job explaining when you might use them.

tip If you create a project that uses multiple pages, Photoshop Elements saves it in Photo Creations (PSE) format, so the image data is not compressed.

- JPEG (Joint Photographic Experts Group) is a standard format for sharing images on the web. This format retains all color information, but it compresses the file size by selectively discarding some image data. The higher the compression, the lower the image quality, and vice versa. Each time you save in JPEG format, the image is compressed again, so you lose more data. That's why it's a good idea to hold off on saving as JPEG until you're done editing your file.

- PNG (Portable Network Graphics) is a newer but popular file format for images on the web. It compresses the image without losing any data, and it can preserve transparency in grayscale and RGB images. Unfortunately, some older web browsers don't recognize PNG images.

- TIFF (Tagged-Image File Format) is a time-tested, high-quality bitmap image format best suited for print. TIFF is a good format to use if you'll be importing the image into a page layout application, for example.

Understanding file compression

File compression can be a valuable thing. It's what makes it possible to share images almost everywhere. But it often requires some compromise. You'll see options for file compression when you save images in TIFF, JPEG, and some other formats.

There are two basic kinds of file compression: lossless and lossy. Lossless compression retains all the image data; lossy compression discards some image data and loses some detail.

You don't need to be a file compression expert to get good results, but it's helpful to recognize a few terms. RLE is a lossless compression technique that reduces file size in images with multiple layers containing transparency. LZW is a common lossless compression technique that works best in images with a large area of a single color. JPEG is a lossy compression technique that gives the best results with photographs. CCITT is for black-and-white images. ZIP is a lossless compression technique best used with images that contain large areas of a single color.

Saving the file

Once you've chosen a file format and file compression, saving the file is pretty easy.

To save your image:

1. Choose File > Save As.

2. Select the format, name, and location for the file. In Windows, you can select to include the new copy in a version set in the Organizer.

3. Click Save.

4. In the file format options dialog box that appears, select the options for your file and click Save.

Figure 9.1 *The options you have depend on the file format you selected.*

Exporting for the web

If you know the web is the destination for your image, you can optimize it as you save it from Photoshop Elements. Optimization compresses images and sets display options specifically for best results viewing on the Internet. As with everything else, there are compromises, but your goal is to attain a file size that is small enough for smooth downloading but large enough to preserve your image quality.

1. Choose File > Save For Web. The Save For Web dialog box lets you preview your image with different file settings, so you can see how they affect the quality of the image.

New image size and resolution   Preview in browser

Figure 9.2 *The Save For Web dialog box.*

2. To use predefined settings, choose a preset from the Preset menu. Or, choose a format from the file format menu (GIF, JPEG, PNG-8, or PNG-24), and experiment with compression and color options.

Under the preview window, you'll find the size of the file using the current optimization settings, and the estimated download time.

The information under the preview window is updated as you make changes to the settings.

How do you choose which format to use? For most cases, JPEG is the best way to save photographs. If your image contains transparency, though, you'll be better off with PNG-24 format, even though they are typically much larger files. If you're working with line art, text, or illustrations with large areas of solid color, use GIF or PNG-8.

tip For JPEGs, the Progressive option displays the image over time in a web browser, so it originally shows up at a low resolution and then at progressively higher resolutions. Some browsers do not support progressive JPEGs.

Creating an animated GIF

You can create a quick and easy animation using layers in Photoshop Elements.

1. Place the images for each frame on separate layers in the Layers panel.

2. Choose File > Save For Web.

3. Select the GIF format.

4. Select Animate.

5. Select looping and frame delay options in the Animation area of the dialog box.

6. Preview in a browser!

- To preview your image at the current optimization settings in a web browser, choose one from the Preview In menu at the lower-right corner of the image window. If the browser you want to use isn't listed there, click the arrow and choose Edit List. Then, click Find All, and when the browsers are listed, click OK.

- To see how the image is likely to look on other computers, click the triangle to the right of the optimized image preview and choose a display option. You can see how it will probably look on a Windows or Mac OS monitor, for example.

Printing individual prints

You can print your masterpiece to your home inkjet or laser printer. The Print dialog box guides you through the process for quality prints. If you want to print glossy or matte photos that feel like professional-quality prints, invest in photo paper that works with your printer.

tip If you're using Windows, you can order professional-quality prints from Shutterfly or Kodak directly from Photoshop Elements. From Mac OS or Windows, you can access professional-quality prints online from vendors ranging from Kodak to Costco. Just visit the site of the vendor you prefer and upload the images when prompted.

To print directly from Photoshop Elements:

1. Save the photos with their edits. You can leave them in PSD format for printing from Photoshop Elements.

2. Choose File > Print. The open photos appear in a column on the left. If you don't want to print one of them, select it and click Remove.

Figures 9.3-9.4 *There are a few different options in the Print dialog box in Windows (left) and Mac OS (right).*

3. Select your printer.

4. Set up the printer:

In Windows, check the Printer Settings section. To change the paper type, print quality, paper tray, or other settings, click Change Settings. (Then, click Advanced Settings to see the print interface provided by your printer, if there are additional settings you'd like to change.) Click OK when you're done there.

In Mac OS, click Page Setup at the bottom of the window, and make sure the settings are correct. If not, change them, and click OK.

5. Select the paper size.

6. In Windows, select Individual Prints for the type of print.

7. Select the print size. If you want to crop the image to fit the photo, select Crop To Fit.

tip If you want to print the photo name, date, or caption; add a border; or prepare it for iron-on transfer, click More Options at the bottom of the dialog box and select the settings in the Printing Choices panel. Then click OK.

8. Preview each image before printing. Click the arrows to scroll through the open images and view each in the preview window. This is your last chance to make changes to the image or the print settings.

9. When you're satisfied with the previews, click Print!

Printing photos from the Organizer (Windows)

The Print dialog box in the Organizer is the same one used in the Editor. To print from the Organizer, select the images you want to print. Then click the Create tab, click Photo Prints, and click Print With Local Printer. You can add photos to the print queue by clicking Add beneath the column of selected images, and then browsing to the photo you want to add.

tip If you don't like navigating through tabs, you can get to the Print dialog box quickly by choosing File > Print.

Purchasing prints (Windows)

If you're using Photoshop Elements for Windows, you can easily order prints, photo books, or other products from Shutterfly or Kodak Gallery. Before you order any photo product, make sure you've optimized your photos and that you've made any edits you want to make. While it can be frustrating to print a photo to your home printer and then realize you didn't clean up some details, it's expensive to realize only after you've had your photo project professionally printed and shipped that you need to make more edits.

note Ordering prints directly from a professional service is not available in Mac OS because Photoshop Elements for Windows uses the Organizer to connect with the service.

To order prints from Editor or Organizer, choose File > Order Prints > Order Shutterfly Prints, or File > Order Prints > Order Kodak Prints. You'll be connected to the service, which walks you through creating an account (or signing in if you already have one), and then selecting and ordering your prints.

tip There are often special promotions for Adobe customers. If you don't already have an account, you might want to look at each service to see what they're offering before making a decision.

Creating projects

You can combine photos to create contact sheets and picture packages for printing, photo books, calendars, greeting cards, and other nifty things. If you're using Windows, you can connect easily to Shutterfly or Kodak Gallery to have many of those creations professionally printed. But you can also print many of them directly to your own printer, whether you're using Windows or Mac OS.

Contact sheets

A contact sheet arranges thumbnails of multiple images on a page for efficient printing and review.

To print a contact sheet from Photoshop Elements in Windows:

1. Select the images you want to use in the Organizer.

2. Choose File > Print.

3. Select Contact Sheet from the Select Type of Print menu.

4. Select a layout.

Figure 9.5
Select a layout for the contact sheet in the Print dialog box.

5. If you want to display the photo date, file name, or caption, select Show Print Options and select the options you want. To add images to the contact sheet, click Add, select the images you want, and then click Done.

6. When the contact sheet preview is satisfactory, make sure your printer settings are appropriate and click Print.

tip You can print a contact sheet to PDF Printer if you have Adobe Acrobat installed, and then send the PDF file via email for others' review.

To print a contact sheet from Photoshop Elements in Mac OS:

1. Choose File > Contact Sheet II.

2. In the Contact Sheet dialog box, select the folder whose images you want to include in the contact sheet (or select Use Current Open Documents), and then select options for the document size and contact sheet layout. You can include the file name as a caption.

Figure 9.6 *On the Mac, use the Contact Sheet dialog box to design the layout of your contact sheet.*

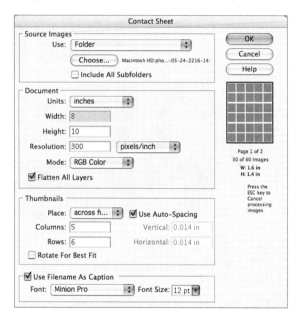

3. Click OK to create the contact sheet. Photoshop Elements processes the images and creates one or more contact sheets (depending on the number of images selected), and adds them to the Project Bin.

4. Print the contact sheet just as you'd print a single photo.

Picture Package

The Picture Package feature prints multiple copies of a photo in different sizes on a single page, similar to the pages of photos sold to parents of schoolchildren.

Figure 9.7 *A picture package puts multiple copies of a single photo on a single page.*

To print a picture package in Windows:

1. Select the photo in the Organizer.

2. Choose File > Print.

3. Select Picture Package from the Select Type Of Print menu.

4. Select a layout option, and a frame style, if you want one. If you have multiple images open, you can restrict the printing to the first photo by selecting Fill Page With First Photo. With that option selected, each photo fills its own page.

5. Check that the printer and paper settings are correct.

6. Click Print.

To print a picture package from Photoshop Elements in Mac OS:

1. Make sure the picture you want to print is active.

2. Choose File > Picture Package.

3. In the Picture Package dialog box, specify the document size and select a layout option.

4. Select label options if you want a label.

5. Click OK. The picture package is added to the Project Bin.

6. Print the picture package as you would an individual photo.

 To customize the layout, click Edit Layout and create your own image zones. You can save the layout for later use.

Other projects

In either version of Photoshop Elements, you can create a photo book, greeting card, or photo collage for printing to your own printer. Click the Create tab, and then click the appropriate button to begin work on your project. (Click More Options to see additional projects, such as CD or DVD jackets.) Photoshop Elements guides you through the project as you select the title page photo, layout options, themes, and other options for your project.

In Windows, you can use services from Shutterfly or Kodak Gallery to create and order professionally printed photo books, greeting cards, and calendars. Just click the appropriate button in the Create tab in the Organizer or the Editor.

Sharing images online

There are numerous ways to share images online, whether you have your own website or are using a photo-sharing website. You can have up to 2 GB of free space for your photos on Photoshop.com. It's easiest to upload photos to Photoshop.com in Windows, but not all that difficult to do so from Mac OS.

Sharing on Photoshop.com from Windows

The Organizer includes an Online Album wizard that guides you through the process of adding and arranging photos, applying layout templates, and even sharing the files. Online albums are optimized for viewing images on a web page. Once you've created an online album you can share it on Photoshop.com.

To create your album, start by clicking the Share tab in the Organizer or Editor. (You can select Online Album in the Editor, but it will open the Organizer for you to start the wizard.) Click Online Album, select Create New Album, select how you want to share it, and click Next. Add the images you want to include, and name the album.

Then click the Sharing tab. At the top of the left window are a series of templates. To select one, double-click it. You can preview different templates, but it may take a moment for Photoshop Elements to load your images each time. When you've found the template you like, select how you want to share the album. If you're sharing on Photoshop.com, select whether you want to display the album in your gallery and enter the email addresses for anyone you want to notify about the album. If you're export-ing to a DVD, a CD, an FTP site, or a hard drive, fill in additional information. Then click Done.

Figure 9.8
Choose from album templates to arrange your photos for viewers.

Sharing images online from Mac OS

If you're using Photoshop Elements for Mac, you can create a Web Gallery in Adobe Bridge that you can upload to a website. Click the Share tab, and then click Web Photo Gallery. Bridge opens, with the Output panel open. Select a template and style, color palette, and appearance. Enter a title and caption for the gallery in the Site Info section. In the Create Gallery section, click Save To Disk to save the gallery on your hard drive. If you want to upload it to a website, select Upload and enter the FTP server information.

You can share files on Photoshop.com from the Mac, too. Unfortunately, there's no direct way to do this from Photoshop Elements or Bridge. However, you can log in to Photoshop.com and upload individual images into an album.

Index